Fort Duncan, Texas

Rock of the Rio Grande
Line of Defense

Richard A. Thompson (signature)

Richard A. Thompson

NORTEX PRESS   Austin, Texas

FIRST EDITION
Copyright © 2004
By Richard A. Thompson
Printed in the United States of America
By Nortex Press
A Division of Sunbelt Media, Inc.
P.O. Drawer 90159 ⬚ Austin, Texas 78709-0159
email: sales@eakinpress.com
⬚ website: www.eakinpress.com ⬚
ALL RIGHTS RESERVED.

1   2   3   4   5   6   7   8   9
1-57168-534-0

Library of Congress Cataloging-in-Publication Data
Thompson, Richard A. (Richard Alva), 1934–
    Fort Duncan, Texas : rock of the Rio Grande line of defense /
Richard A. Thompson.– 1st ed.
        p.   cm.
    Includes bibliographical references (p.) and index.
    ISBN 1-57168-534-0 (alk. paper)
    1. Fort Duncan (Tex.)—History. 2. Frontier and pioneer life—
Texas—Fort Duncan. 3. Mexican War, 1846-1848—Influence.
4. Mexican War, 1846-1848—Texas. 5. Texas—History—1846-1850.
6. Mexican-American Border Region—History, Military. 7. United
States. Army—Military life—History—19th century. 8. United
States. Army—Military life—History—20th century. I. Title.
F394.F634 T47   2002
355'.009767'09034–dc21   2002010646

Contents

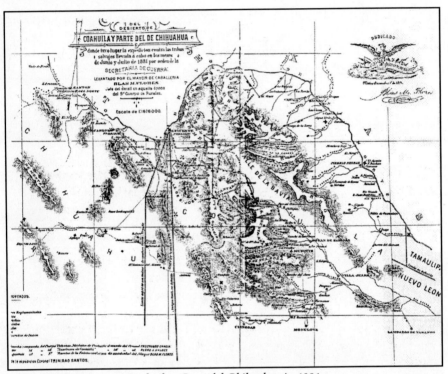

Coahuila y Parte del Chihuahua in 1881.

—Charles G. Downing Collection

Introduction

The remains of Fort Duncan rest uneasily near the banks of the Rio Grande. Bonded in community, the city of Eagle Pass, Texas, now acts as repository and caretaker for a fort long unused as a military site. Its history, largely overlooked, has begged for just and definitive attention.

To the south-southeast, sentinels since creation, Las Siete Lomas (the Seven Hills) stand echelon left from the fort as mute testimony to its existence. Almost identical in size and height, they are finger-like projections guarding the United States boundary by offering security and vision for miles in all directions. The natural process of growth for the needs of Eagle Pass has now removed the tops from these hills and leveled most to accommodate housing for citizens. For nearly a mile downstream the hills protrude, almost reaching the mouth of the Rio Escondido as it drains into the Mexican side of the Rio Grande.

Although both countries, separated by the Rio Grande, have at times been resentful of each other for real and imagined slights, Fort Duncan proved to be a blessing. Soldiers and citizens of both republics co-mingled with and depended on each other. It is the history of those soldiers that this book describes.

For too long, apathy of space-age generations obscured the

lives of the soldiers and their dependents who lived at the post called Fort Duncan. Theirs was an existence without luxury or praise. After the Civil War, the government pursued the policy of containment for the Indians and assumed the role of police for the incorrigible in towns and villages on the frontier. No wars had been declared since that time, yet many soldiers at distant posts felt the sting of death and injury with none but God to care.

Here, in unashamed narrative and image, is a history of the nation's military might as it was lived at Fort Duncan, Texas. No one can read their story without experiencing emotion. Pride, hardship, terror, disgust, laughter, pain, ignorance, bigotry and yes, stupid blunders, fill these pages. But it is history; and unlike fictional characters conceived by imagination, this is reality with all its flaws and rewards.

Fortune is kind to many of us, and so it is that the author has been many times blessed. Michael James Ritchie, author, historian, educator, and friend, has given time, money, energy, and constant encouragement in the compilation of this material. Likewise, Francisco Barrientos, whose limitless enthusiasm for preservation and display of the Mexican and Indian culture of Eagle Pass and vicinity, has led to statewide recognition. He, too, has searched exhaustively for document, image, or artifact to enhance this history. Both these men have met with the author numerous times over the last few years to augur, argue, and present ideas so vital to the success of our project. The result is the preservation of a military history of Fort Duncan.

Special thanks are necessary to several whose help, although not so dramatic as that of Ritchie and Barrientos, proved indispensable in obtaining much source material.

Charles G. Downing of Fort Clark Springs has spent hours with me in physical examination of the area as well as employing his extensive knowledge and personal library. He also gave to the project considerable artifacts found at or near the fort. His personal efforts along with others in Eagle Pass were greatly responsible for what now remains of the buildings on the fort grounds.

Ben E. Pingenot from Eagle Pass was prominent in saving Fort Duncan. The well-known historian and author graciously opened his personal library and papers for inclusion in this history. His permission to quote from the Zenas R. Bliss papers was most appreciated. Both gentlemen kindly offered criticism, factual changes, and several additions to the bibliography.

The Fort Duncan Restoration Association has from the beginning been most responsive and encouraging by underwriting a portion of this project. Their help was vital in the completion and publication of this history.

Much gratitude is also extended to Robert Hausser of San Antonio, Texas, who has long been a generous contributor and benefactor to the Fort Duncan Restoration Association.

I am deeply indebted to the various libraries used in compiling bibliography, documents, and images. They are: The Center for American History at the University of Texas at Austin; The Texas State Archives at Austin; Main Public Library at San Antonio, Texas; U.S. Army History Museum at Carlisle Barracks in Pennsylvania; United States Military Academy Library, The Smithsonian Institution; The New York Public Library at New York City; The Sul Ross University Library at Alpine, Texas; The Daughters of the Republic of Texas Library at the Alamo, San Antonio, Texas; Library of Congress, Washington, D.C.; and the National Archives and Records at Washington, D.C. Every courtesy was shown by qualified staff who never hesitated in going far beyond their duties. They deserve my special gratitude.

Many more contributed to this success, and to all those not mentioned, you are not forgotten. The combination of sincerity, willingness, and sacrifice are truly worthy of heartfelt appreciation from grateful readers and the author.

Richard A. Thompson
Del Rio, Texas

Col. James Duncan, for whom Fort Duncan is named, circa 1846.
—Fort Duncan Museum

Chapter 1

The Beginnings: 1849–1861

Soon after Texas was annexed, the Mexican War began in earnest. Militia, Volunteers, and Texas Rangers left the state en masse to join the Federal forces. Texas, unprotected, became a veritable orchard of livestock, personal property, and innocent citizens for roaming Indians, thieves, and brigands.

Into this perilous territory came John Allen Veatch, a young man who moved to Texas, married, and was prosperous. He recognized the necessity of State troops and while Texas was still a republic accepted a commission from President Mirabeau B. Lamar. Later, when the war with Mexico escalated, he became a captain in the Texas Mounted Volunteers.[1] He and his men, like similar other groups, maintained law and order as best they could while chasing Indians and bandits.

The border between Texas and Mexico has always been difficult to control, thus inviting miscreants from both sides to plunder and smuggle with relative impunity. Captain Veatch intended to keep the untamed area, near what is now Eagle Pass, safe and protected. His was the first organized, albeit quasi-military, unit to camp along and patrol regularly the Rio Grande at what nearly became Fort Duncan, Texas.

Veatch and his command studied the terrain, climbed slowly

1

down from the hilltops on the Texas side, and set up headquarters across from a ford at the mouth of a Mexican tributary known as the Rio Escondido.[2] Where the small river emptied into the Rio Grande, a well-traveled road stayed in good repair and allowed all manner of men and women to cross the big river into Texas and just as easily recross to Mexico. The road originated in the village of Zaragosa and ran directly to San Antonio, Texas. The worn trail was appropriately known as the "Smugglers Trail."[3]

Captain Veatch was partially successful in his attempt at neutralizing this zone of the border, and his command existed from September 1847 to September 1848. When the Mexican War ended, he abruptly left his adopted home and moved on to California and finally Oregon. Veatch began the practice of medicine, having obtained two years' study prior to moving to Texas. He died in Oregon as physician, educator, and surveyor.[4]

We owe much to the intrepid captain, for he wrote first of a camp at Eagle Pass when no township existed. Soon this camp became a thriving mercantile establishment known as "Campbell's store."[5] Despite the fact that commerce was heavily discouraged by Mexican authorities since the Texas revolution, the ford at the mouth of the Rio Escondido and Rio Grande was active for many years and kept the Texans and Mexicans partners.

The Spaniards built garrisons at many of the river crossings for protection against the Indians, and one of the most commonly used roads was between the presidios at Guerrero, Coahuila, and Monclova Viejo. This road crossed the Rio Escondido a few miles south of the Rio Grande, and there, nestled in large live oak and pecan trees, concentrations of Mexican eagles made their home. Quite naturally, the crossing became known as Paso del Aguila, or Eagle Pass.[6]

Captain Veatch called his camp Eagle Pass for the many flights of eagles moving in and out of the area hunting and then returning to their nests in Mexico. The name would soon move to the U.S. side and attach itself to the village which eventually evolved as a result of Fort Duncan.

The winds of good fortune have nearly always blown favorably for the United States. This was so in the outcome of the Mexican conflict. Victorious, the U.S. enhanced its stature in world politics. Finally, in May 1848, the Senate ratified a treaty between Mexico and the United States and lifted the injunction on secrecy of this document, thus enabling it to be published for public consumption.

The treaty was headed "Treaty of peace, friendship, limits and settlement between the United States of America and the Mexican Republic, concluded at Guadalupe Hidalgo, on the 2nd day of February, in the year 1848."[7] This document, usually referred to as the Treaty of Guadalupe Hidalgo, set up in several articles the necessary aims of both republics. Notable was the establishment of the Rio Grande as the boundary between Mexico and Texas, and the requirement that Mexico would relinquish all claims to Texas.[8] Of equal importance was "Article XI." The United States accepted the fact the territory was inhabited by "savage tribes," but they would "hereafter be under the exclusive control of the government of the United States" and that any incursion into Mexico by these Indians, "shall be forcibly restrained."[9] Further, punishment for these incursions would be equal to those Indians committing crimes in Texas and who originated in Mexico. And finally, no inhabitant of the United States could lawfully purchase any Mexican or foreigner or stolen property captured by Indians inhabiting either republic.[10]

The above ably illustrates the very reasons for U.S. military presence on the Texas border. Although the twenty-eighth state was equal to all others for federal protection against lawlessness and Indian depredation, it would also serve as protector to those traveling for necessary trade and the newfound gold fields in California. The latter particularly, because of a route recently established through Coahuila and Chihuahua, Mexico.

Accordingly, using remnants of the Republic of Texas military thinking in 1843, the federal government determined on a line of forts for Texas to fulfill treaty requirements and citizen protection.

The frontier of Texas, shortly after annexation, began in Cook County near the Red River in the northern part of the state. It moved southerly through the counties of Denton, Tarrant, Ellis, Navarro, McLennon, Bell, Williamson, Travis, Blanco, Gillespie, Kendall, Bexar, Medina and westward to the Rio Grande.[11] The frontier in the western half was greatly unexplored, wild, and uninhabited. Only the very brave or foolhardy continued to push westward. However, their voices were loud, and Manifest Destiny could not be stopped. There can be no dispute the western portion of

Texas was filled with Indians, lawless elements, and legitimate entrepreneurs thirsting for fame and fortune.

The federal government sought a remedy for its protective
services and decided on a line of forts, temporary in nature, with
small cost and few amenities for the men who must garrison them.
The idea was to move these forts westward as the progress of civilization passed them, thereby causing only minimal financial loss as
each post became obsolete.

The War Department addressed the matter and in 1849 set up
its first line of frontier posts. The "Indian Frontier Line" began
with Fort Worth in the north and in a slightly southeastern direction established the forts of Graham, Gates, Groghan, Martin Scott,
Lincoln, Inge, McIntosh, and Duncan, a solid anchor at the Rio
Grande.[12] Fort Duncan and Fort McIntosh at Laredo added two
more permanent posts on the river between Forts Brown at
Brownsville and Bliss at El Paso.

This river line of forts was commonly referred to as "The Rio
Grande Line," [13] and was designed to serve three purposes: first, to
repel any invasion from Mexico; second, to keep Mexican Indians
out of Texas; and third, to keep Texas Indians from crossing into
Mexico.[14] None of the frontier forts were intended for siege (i.e.,
blockhouses) but were instead cantonments—a place to hang one's
hat, if you will.

Once each fort was built, the garrison was kept in the field
scouting and patrolling. The houses for dependents, albeit mostly
officers, provided better accommodation in many cases than that
enjoyed by ranchers or subsequent townsfolk.

By March 1849, the military began to move. A detachment of
the 1st Infantry Regiment, then on the march near San Antonio,
was ordered to proceed to the Rio Grande and set up a camp near
and across from the old presidio, San Juan Bautista. The site chosen
was thirty miles downriver from the present fort. It was found to
be a desolate sand plain, devoid of grass or food but "covered with
starving grasshoppers." [15] The senior captain, Sidney Burbank, absent from the beginning march, was sent hastening to catch up and
assume command. After a hard ride from Austin, Burbank found
his troops and officially became the commander of Companies A,
B and F, 1st Infantry, on March 7, 1849.[16]

All three companies were understrength, with A mustering

thirty enlisted men, B with thirty-two, and F with thirty, including one drummer and one fifer.

Three weeks after leaving San Antonio, Captain Burbank and his command reached the Rio Grande. After receiving permission from General Worth, they moved to better surroundings near the mouth of the Escondido and pitched camp where Captain Veatch had watched for undesirables crossing the river. Tents raised, Captain Burbank wrote immediately to his superiors at San Antonio from "Camp near Eagle Pass Rio Grande, Texas." [17] The report was dated March 30, 1849. The command of less than one hundred men had moved upstream, and on March 27, 1849, on a bench several hundred yards from the brush, it became the "rock" of the Rio Grande line. [18]

Captain Burbank, who regularly commanded B Company, 1st Infantry, had an illustrious and adventuresome career in the army. Originally from Massachusetts, he was appointed to the Military Academy in 1825. Graduation saw him ordered to the 1st Infantry, earning promotions to first lieutenant, October 29, 1836, captain, November 8, 1839, and major, December 8, 1855. At the start of the Civil War he was promoted to lieutenant colonel, 13th Infantry, May 14, 1861, and then to colonel of the 2nd Infantry, September 16, 1862. Burbank served throughout the war and was breveted brigadier general, U.S. Army, "for gallant and meritorious service at the battle of Gettysburg, Pa." [19] The general retired from active service May 1, 1870—forty-five years after taking the oath of allegiance on the plain at West Point. In the interim, aside from founding Fort Duncan, he was a veteran of the Black Hawk War in 1832 and the Florida Indian Wars of 1840-41. Burbank was the 557th graduate of the U.S. Military Academy and died in Kentucky at seventy-five on December 7, 1881. [20]

There were three other officers of that first command on the Rio Grande. [21] Assistant Surgeon George E. Cooper, U.S. Army, from Pennsylvania, was appointed August 28, 1847. He rose to major and surgeon by May 21, 1861, and served with distinction throughout the rebellion, being breveted twice: lieutenant colonel on September 1, 1864, and colonel, March 13, 1865, for "faithful and meritorious service during the war." [22]

Capt. John M. Scott commanded Company A and like Burbank was the only company officer present those first months.

Scott was appointed from Kentucky to the Military Academy in 1830. He, too, was ordered to the 1st Infantry on graduation and earned promotions to first lieutenant, July 7, 1838, and captain, June 18, 1846. He was breveted major, September 23, 1846, for "gallantry and meritorious conduct in the several conflicts at Monterey, Mexico." [23] Scott first led troops in combat during the Florida Indian Wars of 1837-39 before distinguishing himself during the War with Mexico. Barely a year passed after camping near the crossing of eagles when he died at his home in Kentucky on October 26, 1850. Scott was the 826th graduate of the U.S. Military Academy. [24]

Commanding Company F, as its only officer present, was 2nd Lt. Parmenas T. Turnley. Appointed to the Military Academy, Tennessee, in 1842, his graduation assigned him to the 1st Infantry just in time for participation in the Mexican War. His talents earned him regimental quartermaster from March 1, 1846, to July 1, 1852. Promoted to first lieutenant, June 10, 1850, and captain, March 2, 1855, his career was short-lived due to disabilities. [25] Turnley resigned his commission December 31, 1865. He soon became a successful businessman with interests in banking and farming in his home state of Illinois. The 1311th graduate of the U.S. Military Academy died, as the oldest living graduate, at Highland Park, Illinois, at age eighty-nine on April 22, 1911. [26]

The four officers described above are the first to command United States forces at the new post on the Rio Grande and honoring the terms of treaty with the Mexican republic after cessation of hostilities. They deserve the space given and represent the United States Army at its best.

Major General Worth, commanding the Eighth Military Department (Texas, et. al) in 1849, realized the futility of communication for the new fort and wrote Captain Burbank, March 30, instructing him to have "on the 2nd of each month a mounted force to communicate with the nearest post." [27]

At the beginning, the new post housed its troops under canvas. Water was plentiful from the river, and the climate had not shown severity so far. Regular Army routine is not long in coming once some semblance of order takes place. As always, the ever-present paperwork, so vital to any bureaucracy, began to flow with amazing frequency. Following the months since establishment, there were small changes in the post's official designation: April

1849, "Camp on the Rio Grande Texas, near Eagle Pass"; May, June, July and August 1849, "Military Post Rio Grande Texas near Eagle Pass," September 1849, "The Military Post Eagle Pass Texas," and October 1849, "Camp at Eagle Pass Texas."[28]

On May 30, 1849, Col. and Bvt. Brig. Gen. William Selby Harney assumed command of the Eighth Military Department and discontinued the Frontier Rio Grande District, which included Burbank's detachment.[29] Colonel Harney soon relieved Captain Burbank for more pressing matters on June 12, 1849, and the senior officer remaining, Captain Scott, became the second commanding officer of the new post.[30]

November 14, 1849, was a special day for the new camp. Special Order No. 74, Eighth Military Department, officially declared the new post on the Rio Grande as Fort Duncan in honor of Col. James Duncan, late inspector-general, U.S. Army.[31] It was a fitting tribute for his services in the Mexican War, especially in Texas. Colonel Duncan began his army career in the state of New York, from which he was appointed to the Military Academy in 1831. Graduation sent him to the 2nd Artillery Regiment, where he earned promotion to first lieutenant, November 30, 1836, and captain, April 16, 1846. His guns were well used during the war with Mexico, and he was rewarded with a full colonelcy at its ending, jumping to inspector-general, United States Army, to date from January 26, 1849. Well-earned brevets were: major, May 8, 1846, for gallant conduct in the Battle of Palo Alto, Texas; lieutenant colonel, the very next day, for gallantry and highly distinguished conduct in the Battle of Resaca de la Palma, Texas: and colonel for gallant and meritorious conduct in the Battle of Monterrey, Mexico, on September 23, 1846.[32]

Duncan had previously shown great courage during the Florida Indian Wars in 1836-37, where he was wounded in action against the hostiles. His death at age thirty-six cut short a most promising career. The 755th graduate of the U.S. Military Academy was laid to rest in Alabama.[33]

It was with pride and gratitude Bvt. Maj. Gen. George M. Brooke named the southernmost post of the Indian line of forts as a memorial to one so brave and promising. Tainted only with the sadness of so short a life, Col. James Duncan posthumously ensured this fort on the Rio Grande to be as worthy as his name.

Orders   Headquarters 8th Department
No. 74   San Antonio, November 14, 1849
                The military Post at Eagle Pass on the Rio
                Grande will hereinafter be called *Fort Duncan*
                        By order of Bvt. Major General Brooks.
                        Geo. Deas
                        Asst. Adj. Genl.
                        Note: The term *Fort* will be used instead
                                of *Camp* in the designation of the
                                Military Posts of the frontier.
                        Orders No. 74
                                                G.D.[34]

Of great interest is the Military Academy's receipt of gifts from Colonel Duncan's belongings. The United States Army at its West Point museum has several artifacts and memorabilia. Josephine Turner, niece of Colonel Duncan, on June 16, 1909, gave outright his saddle and service sword. Previously she had presented the museum with his personal effects, including a small Spanish text carried during the Mexican War. Colonel Duncan's colors of his battery, carried throughout the campaign, are also on display. A wheel from one of his guns with a ball between the spokes illustrates the fortunes of war for the colonel. Imbedded in the wall of Memorial Hall at West Point are the guns of both Duncan and Ringgold's batteries. Duncan's engagements, cut into the brass of his guns, add a striking historical statement to the old hall.[35]

December 1849 brought Company D, 1st Infantry, to the now officially designated Fort Duncan. At year's end, the garrison consisted of Companies A, B, G, and D. Lieutenant Turnley and Company F had been ordered to Fort Inge, Texas, in October to escort 200 freight wagons to El Paso and posts in that area. However, before leaving on that assignment, Turnley, as acting adjutant, commissary of subsistence, and quartermaster at Fort Duncan, had begun construction of the first buildings at the new post. Timber of any kind other than twisted mesquite was scarce. Abundant sandstone nearby became the material of choice. The 1st Infantry soon became stonecutters, haulers, and masons.[36]

October of 1849 saw work progressing on a storehouse and hospital. Stables would soon require attention as eighty-one horses now stood at Duncan. Some were Mounted Infantry animals while the rest were used as draft.

Turnley's duty as escort ended at the Pecos River, where an escort from El Paso relieved them. He returned to Duncan and spent the month of December working on his building projects. With four companies present, the post was fast becoming a substantial station.[37]

Headquarters of the 1st Infantry was placed at Fort Brown, and the regiment was commanded by Bvt. Lt. Col. Thompson Morris. He and his staff departed Brownsville February 22, 1850, and arrived March 13 at the fort now building anew on the Rio Grande.[38]

Because space was at a premium, all living accommodations were still under canvas. Thompson transferred Company B to Fort McIntosh at Laredo, Texas, and Company D to Fort Inge at Uvalde, Texas.[39] The now two-company post breathed a figurative sigh for the sudden respite from overcrowded facilities.

Highly interesting is the enormous amount of pressure from citizens for escorts on the lower Indian frontier line. Indian depredations and bandit raids brought travel and trade to a virtual standstill. The state had three companies of Rangers or mounted volunteers operating in the vicinity for help in protection.[40] By March 1850, General Brooke requested the governor to expand the number of his volunteer companies, as federal troops were too few and much too far apart to maintain peace.

Accordingly, the governor raised one more company and appointed as captain "Bigfoot" Wallace, whose duty was to operate on both sides of the Medina River from Fort Lincoln, Texas, to Bandera Pass, Texas. Captain McCown, with his company, was to operate from Fort Inge, Texas, on the Leona River to Fort Duncan on the Rio Grande.[41]

Delegations from the Rio Grande area had pleaded with the governor for more protection since the year before, stating that California travelers were being massacred while attempting to reach the gold fields by the Mexican route.

It was reported at Department Headquarters in San Antonio that an escort of four dragoons from Fort Inge to Fort Duncan had been ambushed at the Chacon water hole, and one soldier was killed. The wagon train was lost, and the whole reduced to pandemonium.

Bvt. Lt. Col. William Joseph Hardee, in command at Fort Inge, reported that requests for escorts to Fort Duncan were so numerous, "he had twice been left with only four men on duty." [42]

It was during March 1850 that Congress received from the War Department a report by Lt. William Henry Chase Whiting. That report of a reconnaissance, at the request of the Eighth Military Department and to include Fort Duncan and surrounding area, made recommendations for military activity that were almost heretical in scope. Lieutenant Whiting, who had commanded the expedition that mapped and surveyed a road from San Antonio to El Paso the previous year, was just recently returned from that arduous and dangerous journey. Although he and his party escaped almost certain death by Indians and other calamities, he had managed to view the Davis Mountains of Texas and named Wild Rose Pass and Limpia Canyon near Fort Davis, Texas.

Whiting never received his just due from the army. He graduated first in his class from the Military Academy and as such received the rank of second lieutenant, U.S. Engineers, not spending a year or more as brevet lieutenant as most other new graduates. [43] His command of the 1849 map and survey party is without precedent in its depth and expertise. He died of wounds as a prisoner of war at Governors Island, New York, in 1865 after having risen to the rank of major general, CSA. [44]

However, in 1850, his star was shining from his road triumph. General Brooke at San Antonio needed an expert and unbiased opinion on conditions about Fort Duncan, and he selected Whiting for this important assignment. After a thorough inspection of the borderlands he set forth guidelines for implementation regarding military strategy that, unfortunately, proved too unorthodox for his superiors. Whiting insisted on three military decisions affecting Fort Duncan and the border area: first, replace all infantry with 2,000 mounted troops to be kept constantly in motion; second, punish not only Indian raiders but entire tribes who did not stay within their boundaries; and third, the establishment of outposts "where the Indians live instead of where the citizens live." [45] Obviously this kind of common sense approach was too much for our national representatives, and it may be that Whiting's star began to dim from that report.

During this time Wildcat, the chief and leader of Seminole

Indians, and 200 Seminoles and Kickapoo were traveling south through the state. As alarms were continuous with their passage, Governor Bell sought relief from General Brooke at San Antonio.[46]

Prompted in part by unscrupulous slavers, Bell's pleadings included the apprehension of "Negroes" who were thought to be escaped slaves. The general, believing more important tasks awaited his command, soothed the governor but thought his troops and volunteers were far too busy protecting citizens to indulge in "Negro catching."[47] He did instruct Lieutenant Colonel Morris at Fort Duncan to "detain under guard" any "Negro" trying to pass into Mexico unless they could prove themselves freedmen.

The "forty-niners," having waited for spring, began their migration to the California gold fields, and soon the Mexican route became quite busy. Fort Duncan received a directive on May 11, 1850, from the adjutant general in Washington "to afford protection to immigrants passing to New Mexico and California."[48]

An exceptional diary kept by one of those immigrants gives a fascinating itinerary of his trip from San Antonio to Eagle Pass and the Rio Grande.[49] On April 21, 1850, George Evans and party crossed the international boundary to begin their journey through Mexico. Because of recent rains upstream, the river was swollen and very muddy. "We had to go up this stream to the station occupied as a military station by U.S. troops," where they found a "healthy, clean and gentlemanly set of fellows," he wrote.[50] The Evans party forded the river there, and while all men, horses and mules made it safely across, the swift, stirrup-high water exacted a toll in weapons and accouterments.

May of 1850 found orders to scout the immediate vicinity for coal beds and ascertain their abundance as well as commercial value.[51] May also brought a reply for ordnance (cannon ammunition) for the fort. The correspondence is simple and direct. Ordnance would be forwarded, "as soon as a magazine is constructed."[52]

Reinforcement came to the fort in August 1850 with Company I, 1st Infantry. This company, along with Companies A and F, Headquarters and commanding officer, brought the post to its original strength. By this time, too, the decennial practice of taking census was ready to begin. For future genealogical researches, that census of Fort Duncan, Texas, and Captain Veatch's old crossing at the Escondido will be recorded in an appendix. The census is dated October 18, 1850, and is included under the general heading "Bexar County."[53] Those mentioned are unique in their names and spelling. Probably the census taker was as much at fault as the respondents. (Please note NZ is New Zealand and NB is New Brunswick. It is rather interesting the number of soldiers giving their birthplace as New Zealand. On the other hand, many undoubtedly made up a homeland for various reasons.)

At least two sets of brothers are registered and a questionable father and son. The laundresses are all wives of enlisted men. This census represents all persons found to be residing at Fort Duncan and across from the Rio Escondido in the year 1850.

January 1851 saw a bustling post and the early arrival of citizens who would make their home across the large arroyo from the fort. Many were the reasons for growth about military garrisons, and certainly Fort Duncan was no exception. Trade and protection were always the prime magnet, but exploitation of the soldiers usually produced the majority of the proceeds. Bvt. Lt. Col. Morris retained command of the post and did so with Companies A, D, F and I, 1st Infantry, as his garrison troops.

Early January revealed the extraordinary fear of citizens up and down the Rio Grande regarding Wildcat and his band of Seminole and Kickapoo. Many escaped slaves had joined Wildcat in Florida. Through military channels Washington ordered the commanding officer at Fort Duncan to "forbid him or any of party to cross the Rio Grande."[54] The probability of pressure from pro-slave elements who feared loss of their property was all too obvious. The War Department grew tired of continued requests to deny these Indians the right to cross, and forbade it with the above orders. However, cooler heads at San Antonio prevailed, by February instructing Fort Duncan to allow "Seminole and Kickapoo to cross the Rio Grande to trade."[55]

During this period, records of Indian and bandit transgressions filled the events column of Fort Duncan. Troops were constantly on patrol and rushing to citizen complaints. By April 1851, the horror of atrocities threatened the very existence of all without the protection of the military. Indian depredations did not cease, even momentarily. Finally, orders which were both blunt and fatal were issued to all troops at the post: "All Indians found below the Frontier Line are to be put to death." [56]

Military activity from Fort Duncan was relentless throughout the 1850s and matched the decade of the seventies with troop movements.

May 1851 began with polite and urgent requests from the Mexican government to curtail the ever-increasing lawlessness on the border. The War Department directed, "Commanders of posts on Rio Grande to aid Mexican authorities in repelling American and Mexican outlaws." [57] This was significantly short of allowing ingress on Mexican soil in hot pursuit, but suggested that the military might be more forceful in restraint and thereby living up to treaty agreements.

Of special interest at this time is the court-martial of an officer at Fort Duncan. The outcome is surprising but only reinforces the absolute need for every man on frontier duty.

General Orders	Headquarters of the Army
No. 26	Adjutant General's Office
	Washington, May 12, 1851

1 . . . At the General Court Martial which convened at Fort Duncan, Texas on the 10th day of February, 1851, pursuant to Orders No. 10 of January 30, 1851, from the Headquarters 8th Department, and of which Major P. Morrison, 8th Infantry is President, was arraigned and tried Bvt. 2d Lieutenant Samuel H. Reynolds, of the 1st Regiment of Infantry, on the following charges and specifications:

Charge I:
"Conduct unbecoming an officer and gentlemen."
Specification 1st . . . "In this: That Bvt. 2d Lieutenant Samuel H. Reynolds, of the 1st Regiment of Infantry, did expose himself in a state of intoxication, to the view of soldiers of the garrison and citizens, on, or near the public parade at Fort Duncan, Texas, on or about the 12th day of January, 1851"
Specification 2d . . . "In this; that Bvt. 2d Lieutenant Samuel H. Reynolds, of the 1st Regiment of Infantry, did enter

into a personal conflict, and did fight with Bvt. 2d Lieutenant James McIntosh, of the 1st Regiment of Infantry, in sight of the soldiers of the garrison citizens. This, on, or near the public parade on or about the 12th day of January, 1851, at Fort Duncan, Texas."

Charge II:

"Conduct subversive of good order and military discipline."

Specification 1st . . . "In this: That Bvt. 2d Lieutenant Samuel H. Reynolds, of the 1st Regiment of Infantry, having been ordered into arrest by 1st Lieutenant P. T. Turnley, the officer of the day, agreeably to the 27th article of war, did positively refuse to obey the said arrest. This, at Fort Duncan, Texas, on or about the 12th day of January, 1851." "Breach of arrest."

Specification . . . "In this: That Bvt. 2d Lieutenant Samuel H. Reynolds, of the 1st Regiment of Infantry, having been conducted to his by the officer of the day, 1st Lieutenant P. T. Turnley, and having been ordered by Bvt. Lieutenant Colonel T. Morris, the commanding officer, to remain in his tent, did appear at the retreat parade of his company (I, Infantry). This at Fort Duncan, Texas, on or about the 12th day of January, 1851."

To which charges and specifications the accused pleaded "not guilty."

Findings and Sentence of the Court

After maturely considering the evidence adduced, the Court finds the accused Bvt. 2d Lieutenant Samuel H. Reynolds, of the 1st Regiment of Infantry, as follows:

Charge I.

Of the 1st Specification, "Guilty."

Of the 2d Specification, "Guilty" and "Not Guilty" of the Charge of "Conduct unbecoming an officer and gentleman," but "Guilty, Conduct highly destructive of good order and military discipline."

Charge II.

Of the 1st Specification, "Guilty."

Of the 2d Specification, "Guilty," and "Guilty of the Charge."

The Beginnings: 1849-1861   15

Charge III.
Of the Specification, "Guilty" and "Guilty" of the Charge.
Sentence
And the Court does therefore sentence the accused, Bvt. 2d Lieutenant Samuel H. Reynolds, of the 1st Regiment of Infantry, "To be cashiered." II . . . In conformity with the 6th of the Rules and Articles of War, the proceedings of the General Court Martial in the foregoing case, have been transmitted to the Secretary of War, and by him submitted to the President of the United States.
The following is the decision thereon:

War Department
May 9, 1851.

The sentence of the Court Martial upon Lieutenant Samuel H. Reynolds, is confirmed. In a case involving such serious offences against propriety and military discipline the President feels great reluctance in acceding to the recommendation of the Court to clemency. But as the entire court concur in this recommendation, and in hearing testimony to the previous good character and conduct of this young officer, he does not feel himself at liberty to disregard it. The sentence is therefore mitigated to suspension from rank, pay, and emolument for three months from the date of receipt of this order at the place where the accused may be stationed, and to confinement during the same period to the limits of the post.

C. M. Conrad,
Secretary of War
By Command of Major General Scott:
W. G. Freeman
Assistant Adjutant General[58]

As already stated, this officer was desperately needed. Although his crimes were substantial, his superiors begged for clemency while officially kicking him out of the service.

Admittedly, he graduated next to last in the class of 1849 at the Military Academy and while still a brevet second lieutenant got into trouble at a frontier post. However, just five short months after his sentence he was promoted to second lieutenant. Being from Virginia, Reynolds resigned as first lieutenant in 1861 to become colonel, 31st Virginia Infantry, CSA.[59] Fortunately, this soldier's youthful indiscretions were forgotten when the South called for experienced officers.

At midyear of 1851, a band of Seminole Negroes were camped near the old Spanish presidio, Monclova Viejo, and the pueblo of El Moral, located at the mouth of the San Rodrigo River and the Rio Grande in the Republic of Mexico.[60] Many slavers in Texas were knowledgeable of their whereabouts and because of greed and profit decided to attack them for the purpose of capture and return to the United States. That period gave concern to border Texans for the close proximity of those Seminole Negroes and their allies, the Kickapoo. With pressure from Washington, the Mexican authorities decided to meet with the chiefs of those groups for mutual benefits.

On August 18, 1851, at the *palacio gobierno* (state capitol), Saltillo, Mexico, chiefs of the Mascogos (Mexican term for Seminole-Negroes) and Kickapoo accepted a modest parcel of land farther inland from the international border in exchange for their prowess as military colonists. The government of Mexico gave the chiefs "four sitios de ganado mayor" (a "sitio" being a unit of measure equaling 6.6 square miles) at Nacimiento in the Santa Rosa Mountains of Mexico.[61] The site is a few miles northwest of Muzquiz at the headwaters of the Rio Sabinas and eighty-four miles southwest of Piedras Negras, Mexico, across from Fort Duncan, Texas.

That action eased the citizen complaints, and American officers felt more comfortable with the distance involved; nearness of the Indians, they felt, would inevitably bring armed conflict. American officers, in return, were obliged to reveal intelligence regarding Texas slavers and any attempt by them to capture Mexican Seminole Negroes.

One example occurred November 2, 1851, when the commanding officer at Fort Duncan crossed the Rio Grande and met with his counterpart at the Mexican garrison in Piedras Negras.[62] He advised the Mexican officer that a force of Americans led by Capt. Warren Adams, supposedly an ex-Texas Mounted Volunteer, consisting of seventeen men, was planning on crossing into Mexico, going to Moral, and capturing all the Seminole-Negroes. Shortly after the American officer left, the Mexican garrison and 150

Mexican citizens rode west and intercepted the Americans near Nava, Mexico. Adams and his command were forced to retire in disorder and considerable haste, and for the time being they were frustrated in their thievery.[63]

By September, with the immediate threat of armed provocation between Indian and citizen remote, the governor of Texas and military authorities decided to discharge the remaining companies of Texas Mounted Volunteers. On September 23, 1851, Captains Rip Ford and Bigfoot Wallace mustered their commands at Fort Duncan and were relieved of further duty and mounted service.[64] October brought Capt. Ben McCulloch's company to the post, and they, too, received a discharge.

That fall a detachment from Fort Duncan consisting of one commissioned officer, three noncommissioned officers, and fifteen privates was ordered to escort Bvt. Maj. William Helmsley Emory and his command of topographical engineers to El Paso to continue the boundary survey.[65]

January 1852 saw work progressing on the buildings at Fort Duncan. Still primitive, even by frontier standards, the post began to spread out and assume a distinct personality. Companies D and F, 1st Infantry, comprised the garrison throughout the year interrupted by visiting VIPs and constant patrol.[66]

By fall 1852, the Eighth Military Department, with headquarters at San Antonio, Texas, received a new commander. Col./Bvt. Maj. Gen. Persifor Frazer Smith, a gallant officer with much service during the Mexican War, relieved General Brooke.[67]

Smith made many changes. He moved his headquarters to Corpus Christi, Texas, and from there began a tour of inspection to survey and develop roads and riverways while mapping fords and bridge sites. Capt. George B. McClellan, Corps of Engineers, accompanied Colonel Smith and proved very valuable in his work. Their party began its tour from Corpus Christi, Texas, on October 11, 1852, and moved northwest to San Antonio, crossing the Llano and San Saba rivers, then turned south to visit the new fort on the Las Moras called Fort Clark. The party turned east to Fort Inge, then west to Duncan, and concluded at Fort McIntosh near Laredo.[68]

2nd Lt. Duff C. Green, 3rd Infantry (not to be confused with Oliver Duff Greene), in command of the U.S. Mexican Boundary

Survey on the Rio Grande, arrived at Fort Duncan and was outfitted to examine the Rio Grande from Duncan to San Elizario (twenty miles southeast of El Paso). His return trip took him through northern Mexico, and at Santa Rosa (now Muzquiz) on November 17, 1852, he met Wildcat with his band of Seminoles and Seminole Negro Indians.[69] Duff Green describes Wildcat as insolent, but then, Green was in Wildcat's domain. Lieutenant Green successfully negotiated his way to the Rio Grande and crossed to Fort Duncan November 24, 1852.

Coincidently, at this same time John Horse, titular head of the Seminole Negro Indians, was visiting Piedras Negras, the village surrounding the Mexican garrison across from Fort Duncan. During an encounter with a Texan which some describe as a drunken brawl, John, being notoriously fond of the grape, was shot in the leg and immobilized. The now infamous Captain Adams, living at Eagle Pass, and his band of thieves and cutthroats crossed the international boundary, seized and handcuffed the severely wounded John Horse, and removed him to Eagle Pass. Adams, anxious to recoup his tarnished credibility since the debacle at Nava the year before, made big noise about what he would do to Horse unless sufficient reward was paid. The reward demanded was $500 in gold and twelve young Negroes from the military colony at Nacimiento. Wildcat, without hesitation, crossed the Rio Grande and in an act of humble contrition delivered the gold to Adams, who magnanimously released John Horse. Promising to return quickly with the dozen slaves, Wildcat and John made their way back to Mexico and Nacimiento. They never returned with the balance of the reward.

With much ado over his superlative power play, Adams boasted of his business acumen openly and retold the events to the officers at Fort Duncan. Some of Adams' audience remarked upon the considerable dark stains found on the coins. The doctor at Duncan, after close examination, announced the gold had been liberally washed in human blood. Strange as it was, even among the unsophisticated, this symbolism was not lost. Captain Adams, et al. discussed the situation and decided their nefarious practices would be more profitable at considerable distance from Eagle Pass.[70]

In the new year of 1853, Fort Duncan was the same two-company post and 1st Infantry headquarters that Bvt. Lt. Col.

Thompson Morris still commanded. Enlargement of the post was now a priority. On January 9, 1853, the Eighth Military Department received Col./Bvt. Brig. Gen. William Selby Harney, already having served thirty-three years in the service, as its new commander. The old warrior, with many honors and brevets, would not retire until 1863.[71]

In July of 1853 a new graduate of the Military Academy, Bvt. 2nd Lt. Philip Henry Sheridan, was assigned to Company D, 1st Infantry,[72] and his new station would be Fort Duncan, Texas. However, after graduation leave and duty at the recruit depot, Newport Barracks, Kentucky, it would be the following year before Sheridan arrived on the banks of the Rio Grande.

Much hard service on the frontier prepared him for command at the highest levels during the Civil War.

Between September 1864 and November of that year he received promotion to brigadier general and major general, U.S. Army, both regular rank and not brevets or volunteer commands. Although complimentary in an officer's file, the brevet particularly proved an innocuous award all the same. Of extreme interest is the thanks of the Congress to Sheridan, by joint resolution on February 9, 1865. Major General Sheridan and the officers and men under his command were extended the grateful appreciation of his country for gallantry, courage, and military skill displayed "in the brilliant series of victories achieved by them in the valley of the Shenandoah and especially at Cedar Run . . . which averted a great disaster." Sheridan was awarded his third star, March 4, 1869, and became general of the army with a fourth star, June 1, 1888.[73]

Fort Duncan was now ready to maintain a garrison of almost half a regiment. In September 1853 the command enlarged to include Companies A, D, E, F and H, 1st Infantry, and in October Companies B and L, 3rd Artillery arrived. The aggregate strength of Fort Duncan at year's end stood at 315 enlisted and seventeen officers, still commanded by Bvt. Lt. Col. Morris.[74] Space for infantry, artillery, and dependents filled the entire post, requiring removal of all horses for the mounted infantry.

2nd Lt. T. A. Washington, 1st Infantry, was in command of Company D, his superior officer detached. He found himself responsible for training the company and wrote emergency requests for necessary manuals. Writing the adjutant general of the U.S.

Army, he asked for a copy of "Scott's Infantry Tactics" and a manual on the percussion musket to include the new and improved "Maynards lock." His letter dated February 18, 1853, states, "the company is now for the first time since the War undergoing instruction in the use of the musket, it being heretofore armed with the rifle." [75]

1st Lt. J. B. Plummer, 1st Infantry, was regimental quartermaster and as such was required to furnish headquarters, U.S. Army, with a biennial estimate of expenses for his department at Fort Duncan. The fiscal year began with July 1, 1851–July 1, 1853 while Plummer was RQM. His report includes "18,145 bushels of corn at $1.30 per bushel" and "100 tons of corn fodder at $15 per ton." The estimate was for "102 mules (present number on hand), 10 oxen and 60 horses with allowance for trains and escorts from other posts, etc." Wood required 660 cords at $6.50 per cord, repair of public buildings (already erected at $150), while pay for extra duty men was $1,560. Repair of wagons, $415, transport of officers' baggage, $300, contingencies (capture of deserters), $150 and per diem for court-martials, hire of guides, etc. added up to $1,190. Total amount needed for fiscal year 1851-1852 was $31,733.50; for 1852-1853, $33,501.00. Lieutenant Plummer further reported that since April 1850 the post had erected "two buildings for officers, one of stone and the other of adobe, a magazine, a hospital eighty feet by twenty-five, and finished a store house fifty-four feet by thirty, of two stories." The officers' quarters were built entirely by soldier labor with one hired carpenter, the wood having been hauled from "Ringgold Barracks," South Texas, on the Rio Grande.

By 1852 there were two more frame and mud houses with thatched roofs for officers while most lived in hospital tents, "nearly worn out," and "tents stretched over a wood frame with a pine wood floor." The enlisted men were quartered by company in "6 huts made of poles plastered with mud, grass roofs and floors of mud with no ventilation." Plummer continued that "stone was the only building material the country furnishes." Resignedly, he pointed out "there is not a stick of timber suitable . . . within 70 miles." He also mentioned an "extensive bed of bituminous coal . . . very good quality . . . found on banks of the river about six miles above [Fort Duncan]." [76]

Please refer to Map, Figure F, of Captain Freeman's report to fully appreciate army frontier duty. Those who read these lines cannot comprehend the magnitude of hardship and deprivation lived at Fort Duncan. And they were immeasurably better off than citizens hovering in crude *jacales* in the nearby pueblo of Eagle Pass.

There was a distinct haphazard arrangement of the fort buildings. The parade ground surrounded by other structures seemed out of place and incongruous. The references on the map show starkly the pitiful conditions of most of the mud and grass houses.

One of the best descriptions of Fort Duncan was from Capt./ Bvt. Lt. Col. William Grigsby Freeman. As inspector general he made an inspection of all posts in Texas during 1853. He arrived at Fort Duncan July 27 and carefully examined all facets of the station. Many of his comments are extremely vital to our knowledge of Fort Duncan and will be liberally reported from his official statement.

The post was situated on a plain thirty feet above the river and five hundred yards distant "on the Rio Grande, in latitude 28 degrees 42' 13" North, longitude 100 degrees 1' 48" West, 145 miles W.S.W. of San Antonio, with which it was a weekly mail communication." Above and separated by a deep ravine was the town of Eagle Pass, where there were three or four stores . . . "and eight or ten . . . good buildings . . . mud hovels occupied by the lower order of Mexicans . . . population of 80 to 100 . . . twelve or fifteen Americans." Freeman continues with the information of military garrisons, one directly across the river and the other near Monclova Viejo, some eighteen miles upriver. They were known in 1853 as the "Colony of Guerrero" at Piedras Negras, Mexico, and "Colony of Moral" at El Moral, Mexico. Both garrisons consisted of thirty to one hundred troops, moved recently farther south. He noted the existence of two ferries "near the post, and in low stages of water the Rio Grande is fordable half a mile above."

Because of distance from civilization, literally in wilderness, the land being used for the post had never been purchased or leased. The absentee owner, John Twohig of San Antonio, had recently been made an offer by the quartermaster's department.[77]

Twohig, a merchant and large land holder, lived in San Antonio when he was captured by Mexican general Adrian Woll in 1842. He escaped from Perote Prison and died in 1891, leaving most of his estate ($300,000) to the Catholic Church.

The proposition tendered by the government was to lease the

land for fifteen years with ". . . use of the timber and coal . . . extending three miles up the river." There was an abundance of mesquite for fuel to last the present garrison for five years and plenty of stone "suitable for building but no lumber." An offer of $100 a month for the first five years was made, with one dollar a month thereafter on the condition all buildings and improvements would revert to the owner at expiration of the lease.

Freeman concluded from examination that a better site could have been chosen. His suggestion would have been across from the presidio at Guerrero, thirty miles below the present site and the main San Antonio road used by Santa Anna in 1836 on his way to the Alamo, and by Gen. John E. Wool on his invasion of Mexico in 1846.

Guerrero, touting a population of 1,200, was more civilized and land was comparatively cheap. The site would have also been more equidistant between Forts McIntosh, 110 miles distant, and Clark, 70 miles distant. However, other than distance, very little could be said of one site over the other.

On July 27, 1853, Captain Freeman reviewed and inspected the garrison. The post consisted of Companies D and F, 1st Infantry, commanded by Maj. Thompson Morris. "Field and Staff Maj. T. Morris (Bvt. Lt. Col.), and Asst. Surgeon G. K. Wood; Company D—2nd Lt. T. A. Washington, and 36 men; Company F—2nd Lt. G. A. Williams, and 28 men."

The absent officers were Capt. Seth Eastman, on duty in Washington at the Indian Department, and 1st Lt. Theophile D'oremieuix at the Military Academy, both of Company D, 1st Infantry. Capt. B. H. Arthur, on leave, 1st Lt. Charles Champion Gilbert at the Military Academy, and Lt. Thomas Greenhow Williams, also on leave, were all assigned to Company F, 1st Infantry.

The Freeman report continued by stating the clothing, arms and accouterments were in good order but instruction was quite limited. That he attributed to reduced company strength, "and the heavy details for extra duty," meaning building labor and constant patrols. It was pointed out the enlisted quarters were "not for occupancy." According to Major Morris, no more permanent buildings were to be erected until a lease was obtained. Freeman requested immediate building of new quarters as long as the fort was to be maintained. Since no carpenters, masons, or blacksmiths were in the command, the government had to hire them in order to have livable facilities.

The ordnance at Fort Duncan inspected by Freeman included one six-pounder gun and one twelve-pounder howitzer with their caissons. "No gun shed is finished to shelter this ordnance."

The quartermaster department, ably commanded by Lieutenant Washington, was nowhere near adequate. Although housed in a stone building, the amount of property overflowed. As for the subsistence department, also under Lieutenant Washington, most of the food was purchased in New Orleans, shipped to Corpus Christi, and transported overland by mule train.

Freeman was highly complimentary of Assistant Surgeon Woods and the large stone hospital. Diseases noted involved intemperance and climatic changes. As stated, this resume of Freeman's report is critical to understanding how life was lived and its effects on the garrison in the early 1850s.[79]

January 1854 brought Company C, 1st Artillery to Duncan and the total garrison included Companies A, B, D, E, F, G and H, 1st Infantry. Major Morris, after four years in command, was replaced as commanding officer by Col. Joseph Plympton, promoted to that rank and assignment six months previous.[80] Colonel Plympton had been serving as an officer since January 3, 1812, and had seen much action against Indians during the Mexican War.

The year 1854 brought many notables to Fort Duncan. Its officer ranks would fill both Union and Confederate armies in the war to come. Regimental staff were Colonel Plympton, commanding regiment and post, Maj./Bvt. Lt. Col. T. Morris as executive officer, and Asst. Surgeon George K. Wood as medical officer. The adjutant was 2nd Lt. (later general) Richard W. Johnson, and quartermaster, ably handled by 2nd Lt. (and later general) Samuel Beckley Holabird. The company officers appearing as present in the March 1854 returns were as follows: Captains William E. Prince, E, George W. Wallace, G, Benjamin, H, Arthur, F, James N. Caldwell, A, and Stephen D. Carpenter, Company H. The first lieutenants were: Eugene E. McLean, commanding D, Charles N. Underwood, H, and Andrew G. Miller, commanding B Company. Brevet lieutenants were Henry E. Maynadier, 1st Artillery and commanding Company C of that regiment, James B. Greene, 1st Infantry, B,

Charles R. Woods, G, Peter T. Swaine, E, and George A. Williams, H Company.[81]

Bvt. Lt. Phillip H. Sheridan arrived March 4, 1854, via Corpus Christi and Laredo. He became the nineteenth officer present for duty at Fort Duncan during March.[82]

Sheridan's memoirs, published in two volumes in 1888, describe his arrival at his new post: "The company to which I was attached was quartered at Fort Duncan, a military post on the Rio Grande opposite the little town of Piedras Negras . . ."[83] Either Eagle Pass was not considered (a little town) or time and memory had dimmed its existence. Sheridan, in Kentucky since graduation from West Point, recalled his travel to this frontier post in a most entertaining manner. By steamboat down the Ohio to the Mississippi and then down to New Orleans, he boarded a steamer, crossed the Gulf of Mexico, and landed at the port of Indianola, Texas. Then by schooner he traveled the inner channel or Laguna Madre to Corpus Christi. After paying his respects to the department commander, which was customary, he took leave with a train of government wagons carrying supplies to various posts and headed for Laredo. "There being no other means of reaching my station . . . possessions . . . a trunk, mattress, two blankets and a pillow . . . on a wagon, sitting on the boxes or bags of coffee and sugar . . ." After reaching Fort McIntosh, Sheridan was authorized use of a government six-mule wagon for himself and "possessions" and continued on to Duncan.[84]

Sheridan was assigned to Company D at the post and soon left for field duty at surrounding sub-camps for scouting and patrol. He and many other young officers enjoyed the abundance of game and supplemented their diets with deer, turkey, quail, and antelope. Company D, as well as Companies A, B, E, G and H, left Fort Duncan on May 4, 1854, to take positions at three different locations.[85] They were: the Chacon water hole, twenty-five miles northeast of Duncan on the road to Fort Inge, Las Moras Creek, twelve miles south of Fort Clark and near Spofford, Texas, and Camp La Pena.[86]

The latter has proven a mystery to locate because it could represent a now unknown creek, someone's name, or unusual rock formations. *Pena* is the Spanish word for rock or stone, and the author tends to believe the camp was named for an outcrop or other unusual geologic formation. Sheridan's memoirs called it "Camp La Pena" and placed it "60 or 70 miles east of Fort Duncan." [87]

Sheridan's first camp was at the Chacon, although he and company rotated every few weeks to La Pena throughout the summer and fall. As winter approached, the sub-camps would return to Fort Duncan as the Indians returned to their permanent winter quarters. One of the primary duties in 1854 was to prevent Indian settlement in the Nueces Valley "below a line twenty miles north of the San Antonio-Fort Clark road." [88]

Camp La Pena, the author believes, is near Big Wells, Texas, and one and one-quarter miles above the Nueces River. The area contains several huge limestone projections and in appearance resemble large mushrooms or toadstools. The distance from Fort Duncan matches the "60 or 70 miles," and direction is just south of easterly. (*Author's note*: In my research I spent many months and miles hoping to pinpoint the location. Then, by chance, and the kindness of Mr. and Mrs. John K. Matthews of San Antonio, whose hunting lease includes the rocks, I was permitted to examine and photograph these strange phenomena. Geologically they are called cretions, and those found here are immense and most unusual. The limestone forms are normally less than an inch in height, but because of their enormous size in this location I suggest this to be Camp La Pena.)

Another officer of great ability graduated from the Military Academy in 1854 and was assigned to the 1st Infantry at Fort Duncan. His name was Zenas R. Bliss. As a brevet lieutenant, he and his company, F, were soon in the field at one of the sub-camps. Bliss would return to Fort Duncan after the rebellion and command the post in 1870. On his first arrival Sheridan was his roommate and they built a lifelong friendship while both learned their profession. Hunting was a particularly pleasant pastime, and his unpublished memoirs relate many stories of camp and field. [89]

The regimental adjutant, 2nd Lt. Richard W. Johnson, wrote an autobiography called *A Soldier's Reminiscences in Peace and War*, published in 1886. In it is revealed his stay at Fort Duncan and numerous anecdotes involving himself and others. He mentions the great amount of travel between San Antonio and the interior of Mexico that crosses near Fort Duncan and suggests the post was situated here rather than Guerrero because of that travel. Johnson despised Texas, quite frankly, and his comments are both incisive and vituperative. "It was possibly on a trip to Fort Duncan when General Sheridan declared that if he owned Texas and the infernal regions he would lease the State and reside in the other place." He does appreciate the eastern part of the state but on the frontier, "the people are ignorant, destitute of refinement, and have no respect for law and order." He further stated, "while stationed at Fort Duncan ... one can safely say someone was murdered in Eagle Pass ... every day in the year." Crime was wanton and horse stealing the most serious offense. Murder was considered significantly less serious.[90]

His candid remembrances of Duncan were less than complimentary. Buildings had no reference to each other or direction: "Had they been deposited . . . as result of a cyclone . . . no less regard for regularity or conformity." The house of the commanding officer was of adobe while its neighbor was made of stone. Mud and log houses or tents and tarpaulin stretched over poles quartered the officers in general confusion. Johnson commends the enlisted men as "having the only buildings in line," and they were constructed of mud and grass with thatched roofs. The sutlers store, a place for officers to congregate, was owned by Thomas and E. W. Wallace, brothers of Capt. George Wallace, then stationed at Duncan.

Johnson established good friendships here, his comments to the contrary. The names of Lieutenants Holibird, Eugene Carr of the Mounted Rifles, and W. M. Davant are often mentioned. Sad it was that Davant, young and fearless, drowned while fording the Rio Grande, October 1, 1855. He mentions Sheridan as a promising officer but no more so than a dozen lieutenants at Fort Duncan in 1854.[91]

For Johnson, his "hell" ended with a letter from the War Department dated March 20, 1855. The army was expanding, and Johnson, six years out of West Point and still a second lieutenant, was promoted first lieutenant and transferred to the newly created Second Cavalry Regiment. Its commander was Col. Albert Sidney Johnston and Lt. Col. Robert E. Lee was the executive officer. The secretary of war, who signed Johnson's promotion and transfer, was Jefferson Davis. Only Richard Johnson of the above four served the Union just six years later. It seems ironic, and was mentioned in Johnson's book, that so many of that group of officers at Fort Duncan in 1854-55 would go on to high rank and responsibility during the Civil War. Both Union and Confederate armies saw the services of Fort Duncan "graduates." Johnson admitted that after leaving the Military Academy his only desire was to retire in thirty years with the rank of captain. Civil war changed that for many.[92]

Company E, 1st Infantry left as escort to the Mexican Boundary Commission October 19, 1854, while Sheridan and Company D camped on Turkey Creek, near present Cline Community in Uvalde County. This was an established camp, with good water from a natural spring, and would be used continuously by soldiers and rangers for many years to come.[93]

The author's acquaintance with Drue Duncan, U.S. Border Patrol pilot, in 1988 brought forth an assortment of artifacts found at Fort Duncan. He was also familiar with what he believed to be a military camp found on Elm Creek, a few miles northeast of Eagle Pass. The camp, now located on the Paloma Ranch, had remains of stone foundations, .44 Henry expended cartridges, as well as other calibers, dishes, and other items, indicating a well used cantonment.[94] Until now, this camp was unidentified. However, records of Fort Duncan show a monthly return for October 1854 of Capt. R. S. Granger and Company K, 1st Infantry, "stationed at Camp 26 miles N.E. of Fort Duncan, Texas." [95] From a company of four officers and twenty-eight enlisted men, there were present: three officers, captain, second lieutenant and brevet second lieutenant, two sergeants, three corporals, one musician, and eight privates. The remainder of the company was on detached service with one officer and one enlisted man in arrest or confinement. This camp is truly a find and totally unknown as to origin or purpose until this publication.

At year's end, the Fort Duncan garrison, now with nearly 500, had twenty-seven officers present, the largest complement in its short history.[96] Colonel Plympton still commanded, ably assisted by Major Morris, but Assistant Surgeon Wood was reinforced by Assistant Surgeon Albert J. Meyers, who would later become the "father" of the U.S. Signal Corps and its first commanding officer. His correct name was Albert James Myer (not Meyers). He was appointed from civil life to the army as a medical officer and was promoted to major and chief signal officer, June 27, 1860; colonel, chief signal officer, July 28, 1866; and brigadier general, chief signal officer, June 16, 1880. Myer received brevets of lieutenant colonel,

colonel, and brigadier general for gallantry and meritorious and distinguished service—all as chief signal officer during the Civil War. His was a remarkable career, and his first duty station was Fort Duncan, Texas.[97]

Other officers included Capt. Sidney Burbank, returned to the post he founded five years previous; 1st Lt. Abner Doubleday, 1st Artillery, later Civil War general and alleged originator of the game of baseball; 2nd Lt. Eugene A. Carr, Civil War general and longtime commander of the 5th U.S. Cavalry; and, of course, Bvt. 2nd Lieutenants Sheridan and Zenas Bliss. The following year would see most of those officers promoted, transferred to other regiments and posts, or detached to different staffs and responsibilities.[98]

Records from January 1855 included on post Capt. John G. Walker, commanding Company K, Mounted Rifles, who had reported December 2, 1854, from Fort Inge. The largest garrison in Fort Duncan's history now stood at ten companies with a strength of 500; thirty officers and men. Not until 1914 would this frontier post again boast so large a garrison.[99]

In all fairness to Colonel Plympton, an attempt was made to obtain better living conditions for Fort Duncan. In a letter to the adjutant general, U.S. Army, dated January 23, 1855, he reminded the army that General Smith in 1853 had not made up his mind about a more suitable site and the command was still living in tents. Plympton's pleas for adobe and grass-roof structures, inexpensive, fell on deaf ears, no matter the need for better morale and discipline.[100]

March 1855 was a month of transfer and promotion for several officers. 2nd Lt. E. A. Carr was promoted to first lieutenant and was assigned to the newly created 1st Cavalry Regiment. Sheridan received his promotion to second lieutenant and transferred to the 4th Infantry on March 3. Before he left the post, Sheridan, in his memoirs, related an anecdote concerning one of his duties as a subaltern. Fresh vegetables at Duncan were nil, and a prevention for scurvy was necessary.

... We used the juice of the maguey plant, called pulque, and to obtain a supply of this anti-scorbutic I was often detailed to march the company out about forty miles, cut the plant, load up two or three wagons with the stalks, and carry them to camp. Here the juice was extracted by a rude press, and put in bottles until it fermented and became worse in odor than sulphurated hydrogen. At reveille roll call every morning this fermented liquor was dealt out to the company . . . my capacity . . . to attend . . . and see that the men took their ration of pulque, I always began . . . drinking a cup of the repulsive stuff myself.[101]

Frederick Law Olmstead described Fort Duncan in *A Journey Through Texas* as a cluster of tin-roofed storehouses, rows of white tents with the American flag flying above, and the notes of a bugle sounding clear from the green parade ground. He felt the post was "badly placed," with the hills in the rear as being too difficult to defend but the fort, now seven years old, continued and persevered.

On May 1, 1855, Abner Doubleday was sent as a new captain to the 1st Artillery. With June came much realignment of troops, not only at Fort Duncan but throughout the Department of Texas. Six companies of the old 2nd Dragoons were removed entirely from Texas, and Duncan's 1st Infantry Regiment was scattered between Duncan and Forts McKavett and Belknap to replace the Dragoons. This action now reduced Fort Duncan to Companies B, G, H, and K of the 1st Infantry; Company C, 1st Artillery; and Company K, Mounted Rifles. Bliss and his company were transferred to Fort Chadbourne, Texas, on July 9, 1855.[102]

Slavery was becoming a burning issue, and the amount of lost "property," real or imagined, became a hot debate. At San Antonio, Texas, August 25, 1855, a group of citizens met to condemn the Mexican government for harboring at least "three thousand" Negroes. They petitioned Mexico for return of those "runaway" slaves and threatened strong retaliation unless a settlement was found. The residents of Coahuila, Mexico, responded negatively, not out of moral outrage but instead to maintain their military colonists as buffers to the omnipresent Comanche.[103] The Texans, inflamed, turned to a Texas Ranger to recover their property.

Capt. James H. Callahan was just the ranger strong action demanded. Clandestine meetings were held, and there seems little doubt the good citizens of Texas offered a profitable share from return of "stolen or runaway property."[104] Callahan agreed to the offer and, aware of State superiors, decided on a delayed plan. Ostensibly in the field fighting Indians, his ranging crept ever closer to Eagle Pass and his eventual crossing of the Rio Grande. In the meantime he had successfully recruited mercenaries, cutthroats, some legitimate slave owners, and a few who were simply seeking excitement and adventure. The "invasion" by such a force was ludicrous; his command of rabble, undisciplined and unscrupulous, was condemned to failure at the outset. Near Eagle Pass a crossing was made unmolested on October 2, 1855. Marching directly toward Muzquiz on the San Fernando road, they were met near there by Mexican regular troops and citizens. Defeat of the Texans was not long coming, and a retreat was ordered. Callahan and his men, fighting a delaying action, retraced their march until they reached Piedras Negras, across from Fort Duncan. Here the Mexicans, content with pushing their adversary into the Rio Grande, were suddenly reinforced by an enraged band of Seminoles, Negroes, and Indians. The issue was no longer in doubt, and annihilation of Callahan's command was imminent.

Capt. Sidney Burbank, then commanding Fort Duncan, was made aware of the situation across the river and on behalf of an urgent request by Callahan, lent his might for their escape. His duty, as he saw it, was to allow Callahan to extricate his command from Piedras Negras without further loss of life. The commander made clear that the Texans would be protected as long as they removed themselves to the United States without attempting to bring captives or other property. This being agreeable, Burbank ordered his cannon to the banks of the Rio Grande, put them in battery, and stood to arms.[105]

Neither the Mexicans nor their allies wished confrontation with the U.S. military but firmly kept their pressure on Callahan. It was then that a panoply of events occurred. Piedras Negras was burning. It seems incongruous that a group of foreigners, engaged in mortal combat and their backs literally against the wall, would stop to pillage, plunder and burn, while escape under military protection was scant yards away. Debate with noted scholars is left to others, but this author leans toward the Seminole Negro Indian explanation. They claim the fire was intentionally set by a succession of fire-arrows in order to force the Texans from hiding among the town's buildings and inhabitants. Once into the open the fight would reach its inevitable conclusion without further harm to the village. If nothing else, certainly fire would move the Texans into the river and those not killed would return from whence they came, forever chastised.[106]

Whatever the reason, Callahan and his men, cursing, plunged into the Rio Grande and made for the U.S. side. Although Burbank and his cannon never fired a shot, their presence prevented sure death for the Texans. They would have been summarily executed as invaders, or worse, capture by the Seminoles. Captain Burbank was met with teary-eyed joy from those bedraggled, waterlogged invaders, now rescued. But he also earned the enmity of the Mexican government, and not without justification. The State of Texas thought his deed of heroic proportions, the United States government was noncommittal and Burbank calmly released his cannon from its exercise in readiness. Being an American officer, Burbank reacted to his countryman's dilemma, not for altruistic or religious sentiments, but for the sake of America's prestige and authority. He did not entertain Callahan's mission as objective but merely answered the call of American citizenry in need of assistance.[107]

It was during 1855 and 1856 that the U.S. Mexican Boundary Survey was completed and laid before President Franklin Pierce.[108] Congress received the report of the first of two volumes on August 1, 1856. When one reads the personal account of Major Emory's prodigious feat, it is truly a wonder the work was ever completed. Emory was lied to by Administration officials, funds were not voted or withheld, or were sent to dishonest officials, and mutiny by disgruntled employees at El Paso in early 1852 almost cost Emory his life as he put down the riot.[109] He reached Fort Duncan in the fall of 1852 and went into camp awaiting funds after earlier government checks bounced. No merchant in Eagle Pass would cash Emory's drafts as the word had spread that his checks had been protested up and down the boundary line.

On October 30, 1852, Emory urgently wrote the Secretary of the Interior asking for $20,000 in cash and another $30,000 placed to his credit at Fort Brown or New Orleans. Not until the spring of 1853 did Emory and party begin to assemble to complete the survey of the Rio Grande. After four commissioners had come and gone, Major Emory was appointed U.S. commissioner on the Boundary Survey by the president on August 15, 1854.[110]

Emory describes Fort Duncan as 500 miles from the gulf, "measured by the sinuosities of the river," but only 208 miles by direct line. He wrote: ". . . Eagle Pass adjoins the fort and has some trade," and noted that the military colony across from the post is called Piedras Negras because of coal found nearby. The report tells of Lieutenant Green's travel from El Paso to Fort Duncan via Muzquiz in Mexico. The official location of Fort Duncan was Latitude 28 degrees 42' 16.4" and Longitude 100 degrees 30' 19.3". This was determined from the flagstaff at the post using the longitude taken by Emory and latitude taken by Lieutenant Michler, U.S. Topographical Engineers (1852). Michler used the sextant and Emory the moon's culminations. The altitude of the fort was determined at 1461.0 feet by barometric measure. Emory's accomplishment was amazing as was his patience, but his results are still used today.[111]

By November 1855, the garrison at Duncan was again expanded. Three companies of the 5th Infantry under Capt./Bvt. Lt. Col. Daniel Ruggles took station at the old crossing adjacent to the Escondido on the San Antonio-San Fernando road. One month later the command struck their tents and marched to Fort Clark on the Las Moras.[112]

The year ended with Captain Burbank in command at Fort Duncan and a garrison consisting of Companies B and G, 1st Infantry, and Company C, 1st Artillery. Company K of the Mounted Rifles was on detached service. This contingent formed the basis for Duncan until Burbank received his long overdue promotion to major and transfer to the 2nd Infantry on March 27, 1856.[113] His departure was brief as he returned the following year to again command the post.

Col. Joseph King Fenno Mansfield, inspector general of the U.S. Army, visited Fort Duncan, May 28, 29 and 30, 1856. His inspection report is of immense value for its clarity and descriptions.[114] At this time the garrison was reported as consisting of seven officers, 349 men, one assistant surgeon, and one ordnance sergeant. The post boasted a stone guard house, a bakery, a stone magazine with shingled roof, and an amalgam of tents, stone quarters, and *jacales*. (*Jacales* consisted of poles plastered with mud, thatched roofs, mud floors, and one opening for an entrance.) Three companies were housed in stone buildings and two still remained in tents and *jacales*. Interestingly, Company C, Artillery, had a stone kitchen paid for by the men.

The hospital was of stone with a shingled roof but open windows with only a cloth for protection from the elements. Mansfield recommended plastering a ceiling and dead room and mess room. Window panes were essential. All in all the sick had been well cared for and slept in iron beds on a wooden floor. The hospital records indicated 175 cases of illness and 10 deaths for a one-year period, 1855-56.[115]

Ten laundresses served the men, and there were twenty-eight civilians on the post payroll. These employees included one guide at $45 and rations, one saddler, one clerk, carpenters, two masons, one blacksmith, eleven teamsters, and nine laborers. Transport was confined to eleven wagons, one worthless ambulance, eighty mules, three horses, and three horse carts.[116]

The artillery had been increased by four 24-pounder iron guns and two 8-inch howitzers. The latter were kept under tarpaulins and it was recommended the large 24-pounders be dismounted in order to save the carriages. Ammunition for all weapons was adequate.

Corn was purchased at eighty cents a bushel, fresh beef at eight cents a pound, and beans at three dollars the bushel, all well stored. Flour and pork brought from Corpus Christi was usually bad and spoiled easily in the Texas climate. There were several outbuildings for multi-purposes, and Mansfield concluded the post was adequately served by its government. He made a hit with enlisted men by strongly recommending an easily washed jacket of light material to replace the heavy wool uniform coat then in current issue.

The post was commanded by Capt./Bvt. Lt. Col. Andrew Porter, Mounted Rifles. His staff consisted of Asst. Surgeon A. J. Myer and Ord. Sgt. Thomas Drury. His command included Company F, Mounted Rifles (he being the only officer present) with forty-five men and fifty-four serviceable horses: Company B, Mounted Rifles, Capt. Thomas Claiborne commanding and only officer present with forty-five men and fifty-four horses; Company C, 1st Artillery, 1st Lt. James Watts Robinson commanding and 2nd Lt. Walworth Jenkins as acting quartermaster and commissary subsistence with forty-nine men; Company G, 1st Infantry, 2nd Lt. James Powell commanding and only officer present with forty-three men; and Company B, 1st Infantry, 2nd Lt. Walter Jones commanding with thirty-eight men. All companies were in good order, although in need of both officers and equipment.[117]

Shortly after Mansfield's visit in July 1856, the companies of Mounted Rifles were transferred to New Mexico as the Indian menace seemed to be lessening near Fort Duncan.

Maj. Sidney Burbank, 2nd Infantry, managed a transfer and return to his longtime unit, the 1st Infantry, in 1856 and again was posted to Fort Duncan. In January 1857, Burbank commanded the post and a company of the newly created 2nd Cavalry Regiment under the able leadership of Capt. Albert Gallatin Brackett.[118] This unit remained constantly in the saddle scouting between Forts Duncan and McIntosh.

It was Brackett who established a semi-permanent camp on the Sabinal River, Texas, just west of the present Highway 90 crossing today. The remains of buildings with tall chimneys were in evidence until the 1980s, when age and a new road took its toll. The camp was on the north side of the present highway while the commemorative stone was moved to the south side as the new roadway was built.[119]

More permanent structures for Fort Duncan were still being argued, and for the first time necessity demanded hiring a grass thatcher. Spring 1857 saw Jesus Maria Gonzales of Eagle Pass on the post payroll as the permanent thatcher for the munificent sum of $10.00 per month.[120]

By June 1857, Headquarters, 1st Infantry returned to Fort Duncan and attempted to reoccupy old and dilapidated buildings—dwellings that had long outlived their usefulness. It is a curiosity that the fort, proven in hardship and privation, would continue in the role of government stepchild. The preceding eight years' reputation for success in fending the hostiles, both Indian and bandit, had still not convinced military hierarchy of the need for permanence.

The 1st Infantry, with their mounted companies, Mounted Rifles, and now in 1857 the 2nd Cavalry, had consistently shown results in frontier protection, and the growing village of Eagle Pass was sufficient reminder of the soldiers' effectiveness.

Civilization crept slowly for this area in Texas and like four others was incorporated into counties during 1856. The new county was called Maverick, named for Samuel Maverick, prominent businessman and property owner and a hero of the Texas Revolution. His name was attached to a portion of Kinney County when it was broken up, and engulfed the Eagle Pass-Fort Duncan area.[121]

In 1857, Frederick Groos with brothers Carl and Gustav began a general merchandise business in Eagle Pass after establishing a thriving freight concern moving military supplies to the garrison at Fort Duncan. He started without equipment or employees, but like all successful entrepreneurs he saw the potential in servicing the military and immediately recognized that vast potential. Acting quickly, Groos bought several of the large two-wheeled freight carts pulled by oxen and persuaded Mexican families from the interior to share in the new business.

It took twenty-three days for a round trip between San Antonio and Fort Duncan. He advanced each head of household two carts and two yoke of oxen, to be paid for from the profits.[122] One such man who moved to Eagle Pass to participate in this unprecedented venture was Refugio San Miguel. At age twenty-three he married the thirteen-year-old daughter of another participating family named Aldrete. Their union soon brought babies, but Eagle Pass was without church or clergy for baptism. The families prevailed on the commanding officer at Fort Duncan for this necessity and were granted a building for a chapel. With a Mexican priest as celebrant, in March 1860, Trinidad San Miguel, first son born to Refugio and Rita San Miguel, was duly baptized as the very first at Fort Duncan, Texas.[123] The stone building used at the post was thereafter designated the chapel and used as such by soldier and citizen.

The garrison started 1858 with two companies of the 1st Infantry under the command of Maj. Sidney Burbank. Companies B and G remained alone throughout the year with occasional visits from the units of cavalry operating in the region. The post, still not considered permanent, was fast becoming obsolete. This southernmost of the Indian line of defense and rock of the Rio Grande line was thought to have outlived its time and usefulness. However, once more, Headquarters, 1st Infantry, moved into the post. By January 1859, the garrison was home to Headquarters and Companies A, D, F, G and I, 1st Infantry.[124]

Major Burbank relinquished the command to Lt. Col. Gouverneur Morris, 1st Infantry (unrelated to the earlier commandant, Thompson Morris). Here was another old soldier, who attended the Military Academy from 1818 to 1822. He did not graduate but was appointed a second lieutenant in 1824. Morris saw action in the Mexican War and received two brevets for gallantry at the battles of Palo Alto and Resaca de la Palma, Texas. His promotion to lieutenant colonel in 1857 was long overdue, but he served his country well until retirement just prior to the rebellion.[125]

The garrison lived in the still temporary grass-roofed adobe and tent structures amid a few stone buildings until June 1859. The Department of Texas, unable to lease the property and accepting the further progression of civilization, decided rather prematurely to abandon the post. War clouds were ominous and darkening when the Department drafted Special Orders No. 38 on May 31, 1859.[126] Their purpose was to specifically close Fort Duncan as a military encampment. Lietenant Colonel Morris ordered the national flag lowered and cased and with Company A, 1st Infantry, abandoned the post on June 11, 1859. Their new station was Camp Verde, Texas, near Bandera and home to the famous camel experiment.[127]

The other four companies had, during the five months prior, evacuated the fort as space allowed room at other posts. Most camp stores and material were freighted to San Antonio, and the soldiers simply hoisted their personal equipment and marched away.

It is certain the chapel remained in use by Eagle Pass residents as well as other buildings, which afforded far better accommodation than most were accustomed. The elements soon began to decay. The flagpole, now empty, stood forlornly above a weed-choked parade ground. Its once proud flag had offered solace and protection to many and was remarked upon by Mrs. Cazneau and Frederick Olmstead in their reminiscences.

What once had represented the military strength of the nation on the border now lay littered with debris and tumbleweeds. Any usable material was quickly removed or torn down by the nearby residents. All through the summer, fall, and winter of 1859-60, the fort, so needed and busy the last ten years, lay impotent and forgotten.

It is an ill wind that blows no one good, and those of war, like a hurricane, brought a new commander to the Department of Texas. His job was to preserve and maintain the vital avenues of travel and commerce so recently wrested from the wilderness and Indian. Equally important: to the border were the depredations of a Mexican bandit named Juan Cortina. Claiming to take back all territory from the Rio Grande to the Nueces, he crossed the border only to pillage and steal. His operations had been previously concentrated near the gulf but his influence reached the upper reaches of the Rio Grande.

Headquarters of the Army
New York, February 6th, 1860.

General Orders No. 2

Pursuant to instructions from the PRESIDENT OF THE UNITED STATES, Brevet Colonel Robert E. Lee, 2d Cavalry, is hereby assigned to command of the Department of Texas and will repair to the Head Quarters of the Department and assume command according to his rank by brevet.

BY COMMAND OF LIEUTENANT
GENERAL SCOTT:
H.L. Scott
Lieut. Colonel and A.D.C
Acting Assistant Adjutant
General[128]

Although attaining God-like status during the Civil War, Lee was merely a lieutenant colonel in February 1860. He had been jumped from captain to that rank in 1855 when the cavalry was reorganized. His highest rank in the U.S. Army was that of colonel, to which he was promoted March 16, 1861, and transferred to command of the 1st Cavalry Regiment. Lee's outstanding career began at the Military Academy, where he graduated second in his class and the 542nd cadet to do so. He received three brevets during the Mexican War: major, gallantry and meritorious conduct at Cerro Gordo; lieutenant colonel, gallantry and meritorious conduct at Contreras and Churubusco; and colonel, gallantry and meritorious conduct at Chapultepec, where he was wounded in action. Lee's rapid accomplishments sent him back to West Point as its superintendent while just a captain from 1852 to 1855.[129] The promotion to lieutenant colonel sent him to Texas with his regiment. Most of Lee's duties centered at Camp Cooper, northeast of present Abilene, Texas. It must have seemed a godsend to leave that utter wilderness and move to San Antonio to command the Department.

Other historians have suggested Lee was at Fort Duncan in September 1856. He was detailed to sit on a general court-martial at Ringgold Barracks for an officer of long acquaintance. His trip was from Camp Cooper to Ringgold, in the southern tip of Texas, via San Antonio. It seems illogical that rather than proceeding south, at least to Fort McIntosh at Laredo and thence downriver to Rio Grande City, Lee chose to move far west of his course to visit Fort Duncan. Lee reveals this trip was 730 miles long and required twenty-seven days. Obviously, this necessitated covering nearly thirty-one miles a day, much too harsh on animals for an extended period. Further, no mention is made in the monthly returns (including August through December 1856) of Lieutenant Colonel Lee having visited the post. Although historians have cited Lee's "Memos" as having arrived at "Fort Duncan, midday September 18, 1856," it would appear impossible to have done so. Why would he travel so out of the way? Why no mention of his arrival or departure from Fort Duncan? The monthly returns involve all aspects of life at a post, and samples of columns are titled "Alterations since last return, Correspondence, Names of officers and troops *temporarily* at post during month, and Casualty at Post." There is no evidence that is substantiated that proves Lee *ever* visited Fort Duncan. (This will be discussed in more detail regarding his supposed visit in March 1860.)

Brevet Colonel Lee wasted little time in ascertaining the needs of the Department. Almost immediately he ordered Company F, 1st Artillery, then at Fort Clark, to march to Fort Duncan and reoccupy that post. The artillery arrived March 18, 1860, and were soon strengthened by eight enlisted men of the 2nd Cavalry, all commanded by 1st Lt. Henry W. Glosson, 1st Artillery.[130] This disparate garrison did little more than patch holes in the buildings to be used and weeded the parade ground. The occasional practice firing of the cannon effectively "showed the flag" of U.S. military occupation. The few cavalrymen were used for escort duty and a small number of scouts near the fort. The post was in deplorable condition, and only the stone structures showed any semblance of an active station.

The bandit Cortina became very troublesome on the lower Rio Grande, and the new Department commander decided on a personal interest. Lee had reactivated Fort Duncan as a precaution against the bandit's activities and rumors of his whereabouts were up and down the river from the gulf to Eagle Pass. Lee determined to pursue, arrest, or terminate the bandit's exposure by coordinating troop efforts personally in the field. Accordingly, with an escort of 2nd Cavalry commanded by Capt. Albert G. Brackett, Lee left San Antonio at noon, March 15, 1860, and headed for Forts Brown and Ringgold in the valley.[131] His first camp was on the Medina River, where a report suggested Cortina was planning to reach Eagle Pass imminently. Anxious to put a stop to further depredations and ease the fears of border residents, Lee altered his southward course and angled toward Eagle Pass. On March 20, 1860, unable to confirm reports of Cortina nearing the area, Lee resumed his march to Ringgold Barracks, arriving March 31, 1860.[132]

There seems to be some confusion and certainly a large amount of imagined pride in a legend concerning Lee visiting Fort Duncan. Unfortunately for legend and many historians, Lee never was at the fort. The author realizes generations of Eagle Pass citizens, writers, students, and scholars will smirk and rise, like the fabled phoenix to dispute the unthinkable. Only through careful, laborious painstaking examination of any known records does the author commit such blasphemy. It has long been assumed that Lee's visit during the Cortina trouble, albeit one day only, had him staying at the ordnance sergeant's stone building which housed the sergeant and his records. This structure, quaintly known as the "Lee House," sits majestically on the grounds of the city park and near present Eagle Pass Hospital. For several reasons Lee could not have been at Duncan.

The most telling argument for his presence was a letter written by Lee to then governor Sam Houston. This document was dated March 20, 1860, indicating Lee was sure Cortina was nowhere near Eagle Pass or the upper reaches of the Rio Grande, and he was continuing his journey toward Brownsville.[133] Let us now examine the reasons for declaring Lee a "no show." First, the date is but *two days* after the post was reoccupied and known to be in a *ruinous* state—hardly compelling evidence for a Department commander and escort to visit. The fact he arrived at Ringgold Barracks on March 31 eliminates any later date for a visit as the intervening eleven days would have exhausted the travel time. Second, the letter heading is *Headquarters Eagle Pass*—not Fort Duncan. This would have been inexcusable in official correspondence from a military officer of any rank. This omission alone is justification for the author's statement. Third, no evidence of Robert E. Lee visiting Fort Duncan in any capacity is found in the records of Fort Duncan housed at the National Archives in Washington.[134] This omission would be tantamount to total and complete military conspiracy in not announcing the arrival and departure of the commanding officer of the Department of Texas. Rest assured that military records are an absolute and are as complete as any bureaucracy can conceive. Fourth, Captain Brackett, Lee's escort, makes no mention of stopping at or visiting Fort Duncan in his excellent *History of the United States Cavalry*, published in 1865.[135] Fifth, and last, are the comments made by the late Col. Martin Crimmons, noted military historian and writer. In a letter dated July 18, 1941, to Mrs. C. F. Hedrick, Crimmons answers with indisputable authority many questions regarding Robert E. Lee in Texas. He points to an article, "Robert E. Lee in Texas," published in 1929 in *Frontier Times* in which he makes mention of Lee and Fort Duncan. He addresses the errors made by systematically correcting them in the same publication in June 1919, November 1931, June 1932, and September 1932.[136]

Evidentiary articles suggest Brevet Colonel Lee never reached Fort Duncan, either by design or exigency. His letter to Governor Houston is too vague to be taken seriously as to exact whereabouts, but since Captain Brackett not only had served at the post earlier in his career and was well acquainted with the area, it would seem more likely Lee may have been at the old crossing opposite Guerrero. This was the Camino Real and long used as a military crossing and trading route. Lee's letter reassures Houston that commerce and trade continued as usual.[137] This had also been Burbank's camp, before settling near Eagle Pass, and the presidio across the Rio Grande protected the surrounding area and population. It would also have been a keen source of intelligence regarding Cortina's movements. Lee left San Antonio with no intention of going to Fort Duncan as it was far from Cortina's activities. That he altered his route in that direction because of strong rumor seems little doubt, but the closest his command came to Eagle Pass seems to be by fast-riding courier.

Admittedly considerable controversy surrounds the Robert E. Lee presence at Fort Duncan. Certainly arguments are persuasive that Lee visited and spent the night of March 20, 1860 within the fort. It has been noted that Lee wrote to the adjutant general of the U.S. Army, Col. Samuel Cooper, and headed that correspondence "Headquarters, Fort Duncan." That and the fact he was of "good family," although a traitor to his government, seem to be acceptable.

Within this chapter are arguments both for and against Lee being at Fort Duncan. Unless more favorable documentation exists, the author leans against his having been there. The author's final argument: During that era it was *always* customary for a commander on field service to designate his command on or about his intended destination. "Headquarters" meant where the commander was. Many official reports began with "Headquarters in the field near ———." Further, other reports designate "Headquarters in the saddle," obviously specifying a journey toward an objective. Where a commander was at a specific time did not always mean a specific place.

For those who feel Robert E. Lee was at Fort Duncan, sufficient evidence is convincing. For others not so inclined, other evidence supports that premise.

The quartermaster records of Fort Duncan accurately include all expenditures and contracts. The latter appears in a rental for the property, dated June 5, 1860, and paid to John Twohig in the sum of $130.00 per month.[138] This seems to be the first time an agreement had been reached between the army and Mr. Twohig. Although several attempts for leasing were made prior to 1860, nothing had been finalized until then. This report was yearly and coincided with the government's fiscal term. That last official record before the Civil War offers many interesting highlights: "25 buildings make up the post. Nearly all are stone and adobe with thatched roofs. Most are in disrepair except the hospital, commissary storehouse, commanding officers quarters, the magazine and ordnance storeroom."[139] The report explains the poor shape of the post, "abandoned about a year before current troops moved in." Because of the many thatched rooms and the constant need for repair, a thatcher was hired, the same Jesus Gonzales as previous, at $10.00 a month plus $.30 a day for rations. A purchase of 1,200 bundles of thatching grass at $.05 a bundle was recorded on October 31, 1860. Nearly all the shelters and fireplaces and cord wood was purchased in fifty cord lots at $3.50 per cord. This "Abstract of Expenditures" was signed by 1st Lt. Henry W. Glosson, Artillery, AAQM.[140]

On July 2, 1860, General Orders No. 17, United States Army, directed the following: *"Signal Department, Asst. Surgeon Albert J. Myer to be signal officer with rank of major, to fill original vacancy."* [141] (Italics by author.) Thus Myer, one of the first medical officers at Fort Duncan and his first duty station, was another whose fame came later in his career. In 1870 the Signal Corps founded the U.S. Weather Bureau under Myer's direction. Myer retired as a brigadier general, and Fort Myer, Virginia, overlooking Washington, D.C., is named in his honor." [142]

August 1860 saw the garrison expand by adding Company K, Artillery to Company F of the same regiment. Capt. William Henry French commanded the latter company and the post. [143] French was another post commander with outstanding military credentials. He was the 912th graduate of the Military Academy in 1837 and assigned to the artillery branch of that service from which he spent his entire career. French was a veteran of the Florida Indian Wars, 1837-38. He earned two brevets in the Mexican campaign and four during the Civil War, reaching major general of volunteers. French retired as colonel, 4th Artillery, in 1880. [144] His was a long and distinguished career.

The two-company post existed throughout 1860 and in January 1861 the garrison was commanded by 1st Lt. James W. Robinson, 1st Artillery. [145] With war inevitable, the artillery, encumbered by guns and caissons, were removed from border posts before hostilities began. In early February the artillery companies at Fort Duncan were relieved by Company B, 3rd Infantry, Capt. Oliver L. Shephard commanding company and post. [146]

Bvt. Maj. Gen. David E. Twiggs, having replaced Lee as Department commander, was responsible for evacuation of all stations within the Department. Accordingly, he ordered all posts closed and withdrawal of men and material to take place before the State could capture or detain units of the U.S. Army in Texas. This notice to evacuate arrived at Fort Duncan on February 21, 1961, [147] by which time Captain French, having arrived earlier, "departed at three o-clock PM" with his company and those of F, X and L, 1st Artillery, en route for Fort Brown and removal from Texas by sea. It is interesting that Twiggs, much maligned for his part in negotiating with State officials, had been relieved as Department commander in San Antonio on February 21, 1861, by Col. Carlos

Adolphus Waite, 1st Infantry.[148] Waite had been promoted to colonel and command of the 1st Infantry in June of 1860. Brig. Gen. David Emanuel Twiggs, an officer since March 1812 and recipient of a presentation sword given by the U.S. Congress to honor his gallantry during the storming of Monterrey, was dismissed from the army, March 1, 1861. He subsequently became major general, CSA but died shortly thereafter.[149]

Scarcely a year had passed since reactivating Fort Duncan, but war transcended the best-laid plans of Robert E. Lee. Colonel Waite put out Special Order No. 44 on March 8, 1861, ordering total abandonment of Fort Duncan, Texas.[150] This order by command of the Department of Texas reached the post several days later, and Captain Shephard planned his withdrawal. Finally, at midday, March 20, 1861, the last forces of the United States government lowered the flag and "marched smartly out the main gate." Company B, 3rd Infantry, evacuated the post without injury to its standing structures and took up the march for Green Lake, near the port of Indianola, for removal by sea.

Chapter 2

Rebellion and Aftermath, 1861-1868

The evacuation of Fort Duncan, contrary to more popular and romantic reports, was orderly and without any attempt to disrupt or challenge the vacating garrison. These were United States regulars, who were used to hardship, combat, and rapid movement. The artillery would undoubtedly have been fair game and sufficient prize, had a determined force elected to seize them. However, Major French had been given ample time to retire safely toward Brownsville, where federal garrisons at Forts Brown and Ringgold could withstand considerable threat.[1] The infantry remained another month before their orders came to abandon the post.[2] Confederates or secret societies did not hasten or panic Fort Duncan troops. Neither were they intimidated by slavering malcontents from either side of the Rio Grande who may have had selfish interests.[3]

One case of pure romance and high degree of imagination had secret stratagems being brought to Fort Duncan in a spool of thread.[4] Supposedly, this message from a female spy in San Antonio sent Major French and guns in search of coast and succor. That officer's lady was said to have left precious silverware hidden on the post because of lack of space and rapidity of abandonment. These are the embellishments of stories told to over-imaginative youngsters and they, in turn, perpetuated the myth by encouraging its veracity. Solid, factual evidence gives no credence to the story.[5]

Alleged threats from the "Knights of the Golden Circle,"[6] a gang of pseudo-revolutionaries, to steal the post's guns is likewise ridiculous. To suggest this itinerant group of visionaries was in any way responsible for hasty and imprudent evacuation is unworthy of further discussion. The simple facts remain. Texas, through parliamentary procedure, elected to secede and band with other states to form a confederacy.[7] The federal government initiated steps to withdraw its military troops and material before hostilities commenced, and little plunder of usable might or muscle fell to Texas from federal forts.

Abandonment of stationary post property did lend itself to rapid decay and theft. No Confederate Army or platoon, for that matter, entered Fort Duncan by one gate as the blue-clad Union soldiers left by another. Unattended structures of the "haves" soon became requisitioned by "have nots." With no possibility of forfeiture, only a fool would leave perfectly good material to nature and the elements. Fort Duncan, already in grave disrepair and but few permanent buildings, nobly gave to border scavengers all that remained.[8]

Early in March 1861, Texas became part of the Confederacy. Sam Houston, then governor, refused to align with the rebellion and was removed from office.[9] Although the popular vote for secession was 46,129 to 14,697,[10] Eagle Pass voted overwhelmingly to stay with the Union. No doubt this vote stemmed from the large numbers of discharged U.S. soldiers who remained in the area and near the post of Fort Duncan. Marriage to local women and business interests proved beneficial to those espousing the Union.

Texas was placed in the position of not only defending its frontier, over half the state in 1861, but protecting its border, while at the same time raising an army for distant theaters of operation. The state asked for volunteers for the frontier companies. By December 1861, Texas required all men, eighteen to fifty, to register for frontier defense, but it was to be the spring of 1862 before armed irregulars were in the field.[11]

F. R. Lubbock had won election as governor and as such appointed military commanders for the frontier units. John S. Ford assumed the command of the Department of Texas, and James M.

Norris was appointed colonel, commanding the Frontier Regiment, January 1862.[12] It was Norris who selected the posts of the Frontier Regiment, which extended from the Red River in North Texas to the Rio Grande. Fort Duncan became Rio Grande Station, and all posts received names on April 7, 1862. Rio Grande Station was initially commanded by Capt. Thomas Rabb and the post garrisoned by volunteer troops and Texas Rangers until 1864.[13] Another station selected by Norris and manned by Rabb's company was named in his honor. Camp Rabb was located on the road from Uvalde to Eagle Pass at the crossing of Elm Creek in present northeastern Maverick County.[14] These stations of irregular volunteers and rangers on the frontier were eighteen in number and existed until March 1864, when the regiment moved in its entirety to Fort Belknap in Young County.[15] The unit was then transferred to 46th Texas Cavalry and sent to Houston to become part of Smith P. Bankhead's brigade until the end of the war.[16] Although the border continued to suffer, those scattered companies managed to stifle some Indian and bandit depredations before being called for duty in the Confederate Army.[17]

Rio Grande Station boasted little in accommodation. After a year of neglect and thievery before the Texas irregulars moved in, the post was a conglomeration of ruins. The hospital and commissary storehouse were literally all that remained in usable condition, and both required extensive rejuvenation. The rangers and volunteers, teenagers to gray-headed and gray-bearded non-effectives, were subject to a modicum of discipline (most without arms), no training as a unit, and officered by political appointees.[18]

Eagle Pass existed as a struggling village, peopled mostly by Mexicans whose aspiration was daily survival against the elements, Indians, and bandits. Lawlessness was rampant. The only semblance of civilization was the fact that the village was across the river from a Mexican town which served as the last port to export Confederate cotton. The Civil War in border Texas was not history of much prideful nature.

It is apparent that Union sympathizers were numerous, both in Eagle Pass and Piedras Negras. Several attempts at disruption of cotton export and fort harassment were tried, but failure of concentrated effort under forceful officers and disciplined troops made each exercise one of futility.

Very little information exists concerning the post at Eagle Pass under a Confederate banner. Nowhere has it been written that the stars and bars of the southern states floated proudly from the flag-pole where once the stars and stripes had been so prominently flown. The almost total lack of remembrances published of that period must undoubtedly stem from a population with pro-Union sympathies.

The year 1863 is a complete blank, while only anecdotal material can be found of 1864. We do note Rio Grande Station and its pitifully small garrison stood sentinel over bales and bales of cotton destined for Europe via the route through Mexico to the gulf.[19]

Mexico was rather ambiguous in its relations with the Confederate government and often did little more than lip service into breaches of its neutrality. Numerous complaints were directed to Mexico City for harboring Union troops and spies, but nothing of consequence ever changed. In early 1864, Captain Giddings, commanding Rio Grande Station, did involve his force with the Mexican commander at Piedras Negras. Colonel Garza, no doubt with the influence of Unionists, declared a moratorium on cotton importation and very soon the river bottoms were filled with cotton bales.[20] Not only was the cotton exposed to the elements, but also as a medium of exchange for a desperate South, any interruption was catastrophic. Accordingly, Captain Giddings put his men under arms along the banks of the Rio Grande and strongly suggested the port be reopened. Colonel Garza, unused to such challenge, decided discretion to be the better part of valor and hastily decreed the port opened for business.[21]

Reports in 1864 of Capt. James A. Ware, 1st Texas Cavalry, then in command at Rio Grande Station "Headquarters, Fort Duncan," gave further proof of Union harassment. On June 20, 1864, writing to Colonel Ford at San Antonio, Ware revealed an attack on Eagle Pass and the fort. He reported a force of approximately eighty men under the United States flag tried to sack the town. His command of thirty-four men, "half of them unprovided with arms," called for help from the home guard. Ware placed his men at the hospital and storehouse while the home guard, under a Lieutenant Burke, assumed the protection of the customs house and business section of Eagle Pass. The local guard and townsfolk barricaded the streets with cotton bales and with all manner of weapons repulsed the impetuous attack of the Unionists. Ware, while making a reconnaissance in the dark hours before dawn of the 19th, was captured but managed to escape. He did report all the other prisoners were released after their arms were taken, and the attackers broke off contact and returned to Mexico.[22]

This type of incident was repeated several days later, but with the same results. Union officers, using Mexico for sanctuary, continued to confuse and terrorize the inhabitants of both post and Eagle Pass. Casualties remained few on either side, but death and wounds remain serious business to the recipients.

By the beginning of 1865, the South was losing the war and only months remained before total collapse. It was at this time that a seemingly unrelated incident occurred which would prove to have tremendous impact on Fort Duncan and the surrounding area.

Several bands of Kickapoo Indians, rejecting loyalty to the southern cause, began a peaceful migration to Mexico. The Mexicans, long suffering from Apache and Comanche raids, invited the Kickapoo to settle unmolested in Mexico in return for their military prowess against the warlike tribes.[23] By all accounts, those Kickapoo émigrés traveled south toward their new home at no expense to others along the way. However, on January 8, 1865, on a small tributary of the Concho River called Dove Creek, near present San Angelo, Texas, the Kickapoo were wantonly attacked by a combined force of Confederate troops and Texas militia.[24] Numbering 360, the attackers sought to annihilate the Indians, but, instead, were themselves severely beaten. The reasons for the attack were varied, but suffice to say, the glory of Texas and the South suffered irreparable harm. On the other hand, the Indians swore vengeance toward all Texans and thereafter happily carried out murder and mayhem with disastrous results for the next fifteen years. Fort Duncan in the 1870s sent men and horses on many scouts to find and punish those very Indians who made life unfit for people living on the border and especially near the Rio Grande from Laredo to the Pecos.[25]

Abraham Lincoln's tragic death in April 1865 triggered the end to the festering rebellion, and finally the pus of war, death, and destruction drained to but a few drops. Conflict remained for several more weeks, but the Union prevailed. Now would come the shock of defeat and political control with many unsavory episodes.

There were still men at arms who wore the gray uniform of the Confederacy and held aloft the stars and bars of the South. One such man was Gen. Joseph Orville Shelby. From a prominent family in Missouri, he was offered a Union commission at the outset of the Civil War. Instead Shelby chose to command the Missouri Cavalry. These troops were primarily used as raiders and at war's end were stationed in Texas.[26]

When Lee surrendered, Shelby declared his brigade independent and leading a force of near 1,000 foraged across Texas, adding more desperation, confusion, and anger to Texas citizens. Along the way his command would simply confiscate what they needed or wanted. Shelby's brigade was not generally held in great esteem by Texans, no matter how great their service to the Confederacy.[27]

Only hearsay and southern sympathy attracted those Missourians toward Mexico. Preferring the romantic ideal of exile, rather than submission to the United States, they proposed to continue their quest as a unit with either Juarez or Emperor Maximilian. Popular vote was in favor of the emperor, and they crossed the Rio Grande into Piedras Negras and future misadventure.[28]

As his command splashed across the sandbars and shallows of the river, Shelby, in full view of the abandoned and naked flagpole at Fort Duncan-Rio Grande Station, removed the trademark feathered plume from his hat. Calling the standard bearer to him, he removed the flag so dear to them all, found a large stone, then plume, flag, and rock were buried in the sandy bottom of the Rio Grande.[29] Shelby was conscious of the dramatic effect and knew his brigade would never forget this last defiant gesture of the southern cause.

After a hazardous journey to the capitol of Mexico and Maximilian's refusal of their services, the Missouri Raiders, disillusioned, tired of fighting and being unfavorably compared to the French Regulars of the emperor, disbanded. Some became beggars, others died in ignominious barroom brawls or by disease, while the majority turned north and home. Shelby, after a freighting business in Mexico, returned to Missouri in 1868 and died there in 1873.[30] Whether the Shelby incident at the Rio Grande signaled the demise of the Confederacy is moot and relatively short lived in memory or significance.

Again, this post on the Rio Grande, surrounded by the growing town of Eagle Pass, became garrison to the scorpion, rat-

tlesnake, and sticker burr. Stunted brush and mesquite soon mingled with the thick, twelve-foot-high stalks of river cane.
Remaining buildings were raped for whatever usable material could
be salvaged and quickly disappeared with the brushy cocoon, seen
only by forager, wild animal, or domestic livestock from an itinerant Eagle Pass resident.

Carpetbaggers, strangers, and Union troops became commonplace in the Texas capital, Austin. Edmund J. Davis, who had stayed
in Texas for most of the war in the guise of Union spy and provo-
cateur, was rewarded with the governorship of a state in recon-
struction.[31]

Fearful of any assembly of armed men, Union officers were
charged with policing the cities, towns, and frontier. That theirs was
a job for which they were totally incapable is another history lesson.
Demobilization of standing armies in the tens of thousands was fast
underway, and the regulars, who changed hats from active cam-
paigning to police activity, were unsuited and unsympathetic with
their beaten foe. Monies for the military were strangled. Regulars,
resentful of frontier duty, were soon demoralized. Desertions were
commonplace. Harshness of penalty and brutality was all too often
the only effective means of control. Into this chaos entered the lawless, while the Indian served himself a feast of life and property with
impunity. Added to this misery was the ominous buildup of French
troops in Mexico under a ruler with grandiose schemes. Badgered
by his ruthless empress, Carlotta, the effete Maximilian dreamed of
a whole continent under the Tri-Color.

Civilization and Manifest Destiny cannot be stayed. Although
three years of indescribable hardship persisted, the government recognized the enormous responsibility of an expanded Union and
slowly, with tremendous effort, began its most vital function: protection of its citizens. The period of 1865-1868 are years of limbo
in Texas and elsewhere after the war. More sacrifice, death, and destruction was yet to come to the Rio Grande, but Fort Duncan and
its soldiers would play a major role in civilizing border Texas.

Chapter 3

Fighting Indians: 1868-1883

After the war, strength of the United States Army plummeted. Divisions, corps, and armies were discharged wholesale. Regular officers of high command, by virtue of the brevet system, reverted to their official rank prior to brevet promotions. Many still in their mid-twenties were chosen to commands in the new peacetime army. Four officers of immediate concern to the Rio Grande area of Texas were Col. Ranald S. Mackenzie, Lt. Col. William R. Shafter, and 2nd Lts. Henry W. Lawton and John Lapham Bullis.

Under an Act of Congress dated July 28, 1866, the 41st Infantry Regiment was organized.[1] Existing just short of three years (July 28, 1866, to March 3, 1869), this regiment consisted of black soldiers officered by whites. Its first assignment was Baton Rouge, Louisiana, but soon transferred in its entirety to the Rio Grande Valley of Texas and garrisoned Fort Brown and Ringgold Barracks.[2] The new colonel was Mackenzie, 1,967th graduate of the Military Academy and first in his class.[3] Appointed at-large by the president, he "was easily the all-around ablest man" in his class. Called "Mack" by his classmate Morris Schaff, he remembered Mackenzie as being the unquestioned leader of the class which entered in 1858. He was "the manliest, the most distinguished among us all."[4] In three years,

Mackenzie rose to major general of volunteers and brevet brigadier general, U.S. Army, the highest rank attained by any in his class. Breveted seven times during the war for gallantry and wounded six times, Mackenzie very quickly came under the eye of Sheridan, Sherman, and Grant. His natural leadership, innate capabilities, and sense of perfection were prevalent in all his commands.

For reasons already stated, the Department of Texas decided on reactivating Fort Duncan. Reduced to ruinous conditions by disrepair, vandalism, harsh elements, and utter neglect, the post was scarcely more than an official map landmark.[5] Fort Clark, near Brackettville, had been reactivated in 1866 by Company C, 4th U.S. Cavalry, under command of Capt. John Wilcox. Obviously unable to provide sufficient security and with threats, real and imagined, from both sides of the Rio Grande, the military authorities reinforced Wilcox with the 41st Infantry.

On February 5, 1868, news reached Mackenzie at Fort Brown to prepare the regiment for transfer to Forts Duncan and Clark. Lt. Col. William R. Shafter, second in command from inception, was recalled from Ringgold Barracks and with Lieutenant Lawton, the original quartermaster, prepared to march the regiment northwest to their new home.[6] By early March, the 41st Infantry said goodbye to the palms and gulf breezes of lower Texas and headed for the true frontier.

Nondescript villages lay scattered through the brush, with no railroads or telegraph. Eagle Pass and its adjacent fort proved no exception. After an exhausting march, the regiment, including headquarters and dependents, reached the decayed remains of Fort Duncan on March 23, 1868. Special Order #3, District of Texas, officially reopened the fort and directed that the name of its pre-Civil War existence be once more placed in the records of active posts.[7]

General Sheridan had previously been ordered to the border on May 17, 1865, to ascertain the need for American troops. The large question at that time seemed to be discouraging ex-Confederates, vis Shelby, from negotiating an armed presence in Mexico for the purpose of further war. With the rapid disorganization of Shelby's command and a tired and ravaged South, the threat of invasion by distaff Confederates and French regulars of Maximilian quickly retreated, and Sheridan took his leave of Eagle

Pass until 1873.[8] As previously stated, the old post on the river was not reoccupied by Federal troops until 1868.

Lieutenant Colonel Shafter had served with notable distinction throughout the war. A Michigander, he entered service as a first lieutenant, 7th Michigan Infantry, in 1861. He was awarded the Medal of Honor for most distinguished gallantry at Fair Oaks, Virginia, where "although wounded, he remained on the field until the close of the engagement."[9] His efforts during the war proved exemplary and he was mustered out of the Volunteer service as a brevet brigadier general in 1865. His reputation as a distinguished soldier and inspiring leader led to his appointment as lieutenant colonel of the 41st Infantry in 1866. He served in this subordinate position until a colonelcy was awarded in the 1st Infantry in 1879 and finally brigadier general, U.S. Army, in 1897. From the latter position Shafter was promoted to major general, U.S. Volunteers, and commanded the expeditionary forces in Cuba during the very short Spanish-American War.[10] Bellicose and profane, with a tendency to corpulence and obesity, Shafter proved himself a soldier's soldier while continuously ruffling the feathers of his more urbane and militarily rigid superiors. Shafter was highly successful in his role of subordinate to Mackenzie and later Colonel Doubleday during his stay in Texas. His friendship with the high-strung Mackenzie generally led to a calming effect, and he was of immeasurable assistance during the Indian campaign in border Texas and the plains to the west.[11]

1st Lt. Henry Ware Lawton enlisted as a sergeant in the 9th Indiana Infantry in 1861 but quickly rose to lieutenant colonel in the 30th Indiana Infantry by the close of 1864. He was breveted colonel of volunteers at war's end.[12] Reputation lingered and he sought and received appointment as a second lieutenant in the 41st Infantry. It was here that Mackenzie and Shafter recognized his immense talents as a quartermaster. Tireless, innovative, imaginative, Lawton fearlessly handled that extremely important staff position in three different regiments: 41st Infantry, 24th Infantry, and 4th Cavalry. He was conspicuous for excellence in that natural forte and was recognized as the best regimental quartermaster in the service during the 1870s.[13]

Lawton was instrumental in the capture of Geronimo, when as

a captain, 4th Cavalry, he was hand picked by General Miles to command a flying column into Mexico to either capture or kill the elusive Apache and his small band of hostiles. Even though he was seriously ill at times, his persistence was rewarded by transfer to Washington as inspector general, U.S. Army, and promotion to major in 1888. Promotion to lieutenant colonel and colonel, inspector general by 1898 prompted his promotion to brigadier general and finally major general, U.S. Volunteers,[14] in the Spanish-American War. He served under Shafter in Cuba, then was sent to the Philippines, where he was killed in action at San Mateo, December 19, 1899.[15]

2nd Lt. John Lapham Bullis enlisted as a corporal in the 126th New York Infantry in August 1862. He rose to captain by the end of the Civil War but wished to remain in the service and accepted a commission in the 41st Infantry in 1867. When this regiment merged with the 38th Infantry to form the 24th Infantry, Bullis followed Mackenzie, Shafter, and Lawton into a quartet of most distinguished service to Texas and especially to Fort Duncan.[16]

Bullis' exploits as chief of scouts at both Forts Duncan and Clark prompted the citizens of Kinney County, Texas, to raise money for a presentation sword of magnificent design and workmanship in appreciation for his outstanding service. His command of the Seminole Negro Indian Scouts was legendary and approached the apocryphal. He spent sixteen years as a solitary officer surrounded by his beloved scouts, whose story would fill a complete volume. Bullis received his majority in 1887 and was rewarded as paymaster. He retired at Fort Sam Houston, Texas, in San Antonio as a brigadier general. The promotion to general officer was by command of President Theodore Roosevelt jumping two grades in his respect for Bullis. His two brevets for action against Indians in Mexico remain unprecedented today.[17]

Fort Duncan had been garrison to many officers of prominence and high command, but none would outdo those four just described in sacrifice and success. It was to them the federal government entrusted the advance of civilization on a frontier presenting almost insurmountable difficulties. Because of them, Texas, as a state, and the Rio Grande border station at Eagle Pass in particular, owe far more than hitherto received.

Eight companies of the 41st Infantry arrived at Fort Duncan in March 1868. After a brief stay, seven moved on to other posts, mostly Fort Clark near Brackettville.

The first garrison soldiers at newly reactivated Fort Duncan were Company I, 41st Infantry. This company and post was under the command of Capt. F. M. Crandal, but days later, Lieutenant Colonel Shafter settled in with headquarters and assumed command.[18] On his day of arrival Shafter was authorized to organize a company of volunteers, to number one hundred men, for special service in protecting the frontier.

It was a hectic time in border Texas, but Shafter and his troops began rebuilding the old fort while establishing a military presence as a deterrent to Indians and lawlessness. To a great extent, they were successful.

Barely three months after arriving, Shafter sent out a detachment to scout against Indians on June 10, 1868. Those troops returned to Duncan on June 16, without finding their quarry. But they had obtained valuable information regarding the area and its inhabitants.[19]

In the meantime, Shafter was getting into serious trouble.

After the regiment's arduous and tiresome journey to their new station, and finding the most primitive conditions imaginable, Shafter decided a pleasant morale builder was necessary. He granted permission for the enlisted men to have a *fandango*, or party. The only building suitable and still in some degree of repair was the hospital. This would do to hold the event. Shafter next sent the regiment's ambulance across the arroyos to the village of Eagle Pass. This conveyance was nothing more than a wagon pulled by a four-mule team and had a tarpaulin for a cover. Recruiting workers and guests, the wagon carried several loads onto the post and returned them a day later to Eagle Pass. The effect on the troops and their civilian neighbors was substantial.

Alas, several disgruntled officers, already seething from an earlier cursing incident at Ringgold Barracks, prepared charges against Shafter for illegal use of ambulance and hospital. Those charges resulted in a court-of-inquiry (similar to a grand jury) brought at Department Headquarters in San Antonio the following January. Although no action was taken against Shafter, thereby exonerating him of criminal intent, his career probably suffered.[20] It was not to

be the last time Shafter and his subordinate officers were in dis-
agreement.

On September 30, 1868, Shafter had a fair-sized command at
Fort Duncan. To Headquarters, 41st Infantry and Company I of
that regiment was added Company K, 41st Infantry, arriving April
1868 from Fort Clark. A much needed mounted unit, Company L,
9th U.S. Cavalry, like the 41st, was made up of black enlisted men
officered by whites. The aggregate strength of garrison, six months
after post Civil War activation, stood at fourteen officers and 201
enlisted.[21]

Company L, 9th U.S. Cavalry, was commanded by Capt. Jacob
C. Degress and had been at Fort Inge, but obvious need sent them
to Duncan, arriving April 16, 1868. It was that company with two
officers and thirty-seven enlisted men who made the first military
expedition from Fort Duncan since the end of the Civil War.

With the cavalry present, albeit only one company with seventeen serviceable horses and twenty-five unserviceable, a blacksmith
was hired at $75.00 a month. His was the first civilian job at the post
since the war. It is not surprising that comments were made each
month through August 1868 regarding inability to mount the full
company of cavalry and the lack of efficiency therefrom.[23]

On August 15, 1868, Col./Bvt. Maj. Gen. Joseph Jones
Reynolds was appointed to command the Fifth Military District
with headquarters at San Antonio.[24]

Colonel Mackenzie, brevet brigadier general who commanded
the 41st Infantry, was president of a general court-martial at
District Headquarters and not until November 28, 1868, did the
colonel and Headquarters finally come together at Fort Clark.

Lieutenant Colonel Shafter, firmly entrenched at Duncan,
hired a post trader and appointed a justice of the peace on
November 15, 1868.

Lt. Charles Parker, 9th Cavalry, was detailed for a scouting
mission on December 7, 1868. He and twenty enlisted men left the
post in search of Indians but returned December 14, with no luck.
By now the men and animals were in such poor condition, Shafter
ordered them to San Antonio for remounts and complete outfit-
ting. Shafter was determined his command at Fort Duncan would
be prepared and ready for field duty as the need arose.

On December 15, 1868, Reynolds was replaced as commander,

5th Military District, by Brig. Gen./Bvt. Maj. Gen. Edward Richard Sprigg Canby. A fine officer, graduate of the Military Academy, as was Reynolds, would be brutally murdered by Modoc Indians at the Lava Beds, California, April 11, 1873.

January 1869 began with more scouting for hostiles by the 9th Cavalry. 2nd Lt. Henry W. Lawton, 41st Infantry, was directed to leave Fort Duncan and assume his duties as regimental quartermaster with the Headquarters staff at Fort Clark. The post at Fort Duncan was now home and garrison for Company K, 41st Infantry and Company L, 9th Cavalry.

In March, Lieutenant Colonel Shafter took the field personally in command of a detachment of the cavalry company and with twenty-two enlisted men scouted much of present Dimmit and Maverick counties. Although they reported no Indians seen, the small command returned to post with four horses, saddles, and bridles recovered from "smugglers." [26] During his absence Fort Duncan was commanded by Capt./Bvt. Brig. Gen. George Blaikie Hoge.

It was March 1869 when consolidation of two infantry regiments, the 38th and 41st, took effect. Under an Act of Congress dated March 3, these two regiments combined creating the new 24th Infantry. (There had been a 24th during the Civil War, and those troops were merged with the 209th, making a new 11th Regiment of Infantry.) [27]

Like the 41st, the new 24th Infantry Regiment comprised black enlisted men and white officers. The new colonel was Mackenzie and for a brief period Shafter in the field chasing Indians; the lieutenant colonel was Bvt. Maj. Gen. Cuvier Grover. The new assignments were dated March 15, 1869, and on Shafter's arrival at Fort Duncan, he was officially assigned as lieutenant colonel of the 24th Infantry on April 14. [28] Lawton was appointed quartermaster by Mackenzie on November 11, 1869. Staff and few company grade officers changed—only the number of the regiment. Shafter was to remain in his subordinate position, first to Mackenzie, then Doubleday, and finally J. H. Potter, until his promotion and transfer in 1879.

It would be December 1869 before the newly numbered regiments would be completed in the realignment. In the meantime Shafter and several companies of the 41st viz 24th returned to the valley area and their old post at Ringgold Barracks. Captain Hoge, still 41st Infantry, stayed on to command Fort Duncan until October 23, when he left for a well-deserved leave of absence. His replacement was the aforementioned Captain DeGress, 9th Cavalry.[29]

A letter from a private citizen (name illegible) written to friends in New York (Dick Furrer and dated May 18, 1869) is most revealing. The stationery, illustrated at top and along the sides with scenes of San Antonio, is extremely interesting. "Drawn from Nature by Erhard Pentenrieder" is discreetly woven into the drawings. The top is a scene titled "Main Plaza San Antonio, Texas" and consists of the San Fernando Cathedral flanked by saloons on either side and disparate groups in front. Included are laden camels, stagecoach, ox-drawn carts, wagons, and horsemen. Down the side are each of the missions, the Menger Hotel, Freemason Hall, galloping camel, and vaquero lassoing a steer and armed with a lance, while another, muleback, quirts his animal. At either side of the Main Plaza stand an Indian with knife and bow and a Mexican soldier with sombrero and a rifle. The subject matter is most relevant but reveals little of the writer, who was presumably a visiting officer. He finds accommodation within the adjutant's office and becomes "good friends with the doctor."

The writer describes the post as "sadly out of repair," and contains about a dozen buildings. This is "a wild and desolate region," he writes, "the soldiers are in tents the officers in stone quarters." The old stone hospital building had been in such pitiful shape, it took months to rebuild, and tents were used to house and care for the sick. Stage time from San Antonio to Fort Duncan on "good roads" was two days. He continues: "the country is dry . . . scarcely any vegetation, . . . few trees, none for 20 miles around the country." Indian raids were said to be bad but there are "frequent scouts after them from here," but, "do not trouble stages." Such it was at Fort Duncan in 1869.[30]

In June 1869, Col. R. S. Mackenzie at Fort Clark ordered Company L, 9th Cavalry to march to Clark with ten days' rations for an expedition against Indians and commanded by Mackenzie.

On June 7, 1869, a provisional battalion from Company's G, L, and M, 9th Cavalry struck the Indians near Pecos River, Texas. Captain Parker with thirty men of Company L from Duncan lost one man killed (shot accidentally) but was able to capture much camp equipage and horses. Two Indians were killed. Captain Parker returned to Fort Duncan on June 28, 1869, after almost a month in the field.[31]

Scouts from Duncan remained constant for the cavalry company. "A corporal and four privates . . . started on a scout on the 22nd (October 1869) and returned on the 27th instant," traveling fifty miles. A scout of one corporal and three privates went to Carrizo on the 23rd, "a distance of 50 miles," and returned the 27th instant. A sergeant and eighteen privates started northwardly in pursuit of Indians on that day.[32]

The end of 1869 found the post with Company K, 24th Infantry, vice 41st Infantry, and Company L, 9th Cavalry. Captain DeGress commanded both the post and his company of cavalry while maintaining "two pieces of field cannon." The garrison began the year 1870 with 150 men and officers. Through May, the soldiers of the 24th labored long and hard in rebuilding and erecting new buildings while the cavalry company continued scouting.

Reassignment of regiments and commanding officer were not long in coming to Fort Duncan. With Shafter gone, no field grade officer, except by brevet, had commanded the post on the Rio Grande. An officer of great repute for his war exploits and a previous brevet lieutenant stationed at the fort in the mid-1850s returned to command. His name was Zenas Randall Bliss. When the Congress combined and realigned the regiments in March 1869, another infantry reorganization took place. The Civil War 25th Infantry Regiment consolidated with the 18th Infantry, then days later combined with the 39th and 40th regiments of infantry to make the 25th.[33]

The first and only major in the regiment for ten years was Bliss. Since his graduation as number 1,671 from the Military Academy in 1854, he remained with the infantry during his career.

Captured in 1861, Bliss was briefly held as a prisoner of war at San Antonio, Texas, but unrepentant, and on parole, accepted the colonelcy of a Volunteer Rhode Island regiment and served throughout the war. He was awarded the Medal of Honor for exceptional conduct at the Battle of Fredericksburg, Virginia, in December 1862 and retired as a major general. He was buried at Washington, D.C., on January 2, 1900.

The 25th Infantry, like the 24th Infantry, which Bliss also commanded later for nearly ten years, was composed of black enlisted men and white officers.[34]

Bliss arrived at Fort Duncan on July 5, 1870, with Companies E and F, 25th Infantry, and assumed command of the post pursuant to "Special Orders 39, Headquarters, Department of Texas." The garrison now consisted of Bliss' troops plus Company K, 24th Infantry and Company L, 9th Cavalry.

His memoirs, unpublished, remain a fountain of information, not only about Bliss, but his activities. Writing about Fort Duncan: "All the old officers' quarters and barracks had completely disappeared—my house was an old stone building which I think was the blacksmith shop before the war—had more rats than any house ever lived in." His wife felt something in her hair one night and terrified, suspected it a scorpion, which were plentiful. Instead, under lantern light and inspection by Bliss, it turned out to be a mouse. Water was brought from the Rio Grande by large water tanks mounted on a wagon chassis and pulled by eight mules. Each house or row of tents had outside a large *olla* (oh-ya), an earthen jug. Into these jugs fresh river water was added daily, not only for washing but also fire safety. The river water, mostly muddy, was cleansed by adding powdered almonds or cornmeal and this settled the mud to the bottom of the jugs.

In one of his reminiscences, Bliss recalls some youthful impressions of Fort Duncan and humorous anecdotes: "Fort Duncan 1854 was one of the gayest as well as one of the largest posts . . . There were four young ladies, two brides and several married ladies . . . They were all fond of parties and dancing." He mentions parties given in Piedras Negras to which the officers were invited, and they in turn invited the Mexicans. He remembers that Mexican girls, when no wagon was available, would cross the river without shoes or stockings then "coolly sit down on the gallery, and put them on." The killing of Mexicans was very frequent, and scarcely attracted any notice. "I never heard of anyone being hanged for murder until several years after the war," Bliss wrote.

Perhaps the most humorous of his young officer days in 1854 involved a New Year's Day artillery salute at midnight. Mexicans across the river thought they were being invaded, and candle lights were seen moving from house to house at Piedras Negras. After the salute the officers and band went to serenade each of the ladies of the garrison and, of course, were invited in for refreshment. As they left each house they surreptitiously took chairs and glasses and deposited them at the next house. Needless to say, New Year's morning brought an odd mixture of furniture among the post families. Bliss admitted he was the instigator of devilment.[35]

The buildings were but three in 1854, and they included hospital, quartermaster storehouse, and magazine.

The rifle companies were in tents, while most officers were in wood picket houses called *jacales*. These were erected by the soldiers, and wooden pickets were "5 to 6 inches" in width with each *jacal* supporting an adobe chimney and thatched roof. Holes were cut for windows, and an earthen floor completed the dwelling. Some of the officers' houses were made completely of thatch. Lieutenant Doubleday's burned very quickly during 1854.[36]

In 1870 none of the above dwellings remained, including the chimneys. As Bliss relates, the old post was rebuilding anew. It was that year that one of the more significant firsts occurred at Fort Duncan. Long hounded by the cries of settlers for protection against ever increased Indian raids, the commanding officer tried valiantly to curtail their gruesome handiwork. Horse and foot soldiers went repeatedly in futile attempts to capture the perpetrators. But, unlike the Indian using years-worn trails and their accumulative expertise, the soldier could not master those skills to trail and bring to justice marauding bands of hostiles. When Bliss took command at Fort Duncan, he quickly realized this inadequacy.

The Seminole Negroes were a unique and well-known quantum. Their story is yet to be told in any great detail—a major loss for historians. However, after several years in Mexico, they existed in three separate bands, the most notable, for this history, being at Nacimiento, Coahuila, eighty miles from Fort Duncan.[37] Their people had grown discontented with Mexico and wished to join relatives in the Indian Territory (Oklahoma).

Selecting a gallant officer with negotiating ability, Bliss sent 1st Lt. and Bvt. Capt. Frank W. Perry, 24th Infantry to Nacimiento in order to recruit scouts for the army. With but a few Tonkawa and Lipans available, the army was stretched too thin between Clark and Duncan to be effective. Scouts had to be available as soon as an atrocity occurred so as to trail the depredators quickly before they escaped.

The leader of the Seminole Negroes at Nacimiento was John Kibbits, or Snake Warrior, a man of some age. Perry and Kibbits met, and an understanding resulted in a treaty, which later turned out to be no treat for the Indians.

Perry, acting on orders from Bliss, was obviously not portfolioed to negotiate a formal treaty between peoples of another country and the United States. What he accomplished was a verbal promise that the government would pay the "able-bodied men's expenses to the U.S. and would furnish them pay, provisions for their families, and *grants of land* in return for their services as scouts." The agreement, unwritten and nonexistent in document, was accepted by Kibbits' band of 150 and they crossed the Rio Grande on July 4, 1870.

Six weeks later, on August 16, eleven scouts were enlisted in the United States Army at the pay of privates of cavalry plus forty cents a day to use their own horses. This enlistment was for six months, at which time they could reenlist or become civilians. The first contingent represented one company of scouts. John Kibbits was appointed sergeant and his son, Bob, a corporal.[40] A year later twenty scouts enlisted from the band of Elijah Daniel, who lived near Matamoros, Mexico, near the southern tip of Texas. In 1872-73, a dozen scouts enlisted from John Horse's band at Laguna Parras, Mexico.

The 1870 census proved some of those scouts were Negroes having intermarried with the Seminoles or were discharged Negro soldiers. (The black regiments were the 24th and 25th Infantry and the 9th and 10th Cavalry.)

The scouts were supplied from the ordnance and stores at Fort Duncan and included the repeating Spencer carbine .50 caliber and by 1873 the Sharps carbine, also .50 caliber, but a single-shot weapon. Although they drew clothing to match privates of cavalry, the Indian blood moved many to modify their uniforms to suit individual tastes. No doubt they probably sported feathers, beads, and leggings, but a purported buffalo-horn war-bonnet was likely someone's imagination.

As in all military organizations, a system of grading took place regarding the scouts. Always adept with their weapons, nevertheless, discipline, military appearance, and clothing were consistently criticized. Major Bliss considered them as "excellent hunters and trackers, and brave . . . splendid fighters."[41] Bliss accepted these men for what they were, thoroughly dependable in crisis, with innate knowledge of Indian ways and the nearby country, and fearless. No Seminole Negro Indian Scout ever lost his life in combat. All the above cover a multitude of sins, and Bliss wisely cautioned his subordinate officers against criticism regarding white men's military customs.

Some degree of difficulty in communication has been suggested. But for the most part, all the scouts spoke Spanish and certainly most understood English even if not practiced with regularity. None of the different scout commanders list language as a barrier or causing any problems with regard to duties.[42]

The scouts and their families moved down on the flats adjacent to the fort, and the western edge was the Rio Grande. This area, a mile downstream from Fort Duncan, was composed of *jacales,* thatch, and shanties of every size and shape. As a clan of unique customs and social mores they lived among themselves, neither knowing nor caring about discrimination. Although the black troops fraternized on occasion, the scouts generally and preferably relied on one another for familial and social intercourse.

Major Bliss appointed 2nd Lieutenant and Bvt. Capt. Henry Field Leggett as the first commander of the fort company of Seminole Negro Indian Scouts (SNIS in official reports).[43] He was an older man for such a junior officer, having served throughout the Civil War and breveted twice for gallantry and meritorious service at Missionary Ridge, Tennessee, and Peach Tree Creek, Georgia.

Training began, and Lieutenant Leggett soon had the initial company of eleven scouts as acclimated to military life as they ever would be.

September 1870, hot and dry, was spent in constant patrols by troops at Fort Duncan. The Record of Events indicates "Sept. 5, Sergeant Porter, 24th Inf. and detachment returned from scout." And September 12, "Lieutenant Kelleher returned to post from scout." On September 22, Lieutenant Dominick left post on scout. On September 23, Captain Overmann, U.S. Engineers, arrived at post and "laid off reservation." (Finally, specific geographical area.) On September 26, "General Court Martial convened . . . S.O. Department of Texas."[40]

The original eleven Seminole Negro Indian Scouts were "John Kibbits (sixty years old; born Florida; head chief of Seminole Negroes succeeding John Horse; nearly six feet tall; only one of Seminole Negroes who had an Indian name, as far as the records go, which was sit-tee-tos-to-nach-y, meaning Tearing Warrior-Snake Warrior); Bobby Kibbitts (son of John, born in Arkansas, twenty years old);[45] Joe Dixie (nineteen years old, born in Mexico, surname given by enlisting officer, Lt. Frank Perry); Dindie Factor (born in Arkansas, tall at nearly six feet, twenty-one years old); Hardy Factor (born in Florida); Pompey Factor (sixteen years old, awarded Medal of Honor for battle with Comanche and helping to rescue his officer); Lt. John L. Bullis (on April 16, 1875, near Pecos River, Texas); Adam Fay (born in Mexico, eighteen years old); John Thompson (born in Mexico, eighteen); John Ward (born Mexico, twenty, awarded Medal of Honor May 28, 1875, for "gallantry in action with Indians," see P. Factor); George Washington (born Arkansas, twenty-one); and John Wood (sixty years old, a.k.a. Picayune John because of diminutive stature; of the few who deserted November 28, 1870, it was said by other scouts, "John Wood didn't really desert; he was an old man and didn't know what the army was all about. He just got tired and went home").

October, November, and December 1870 were likewise filled with constant scouts. The SNIS showed up as a unit of one company for the first time officially, in the December post returns.

Bliss went briefly to Fort Clark that December but returned in January 1871 to take command of Fort Duncan until the spring of 1872. The garrison at year's end, 1870, consisted of Company K, 24th Infantry; Company E, 25th Infantry; and the hard-riding Company L, 9th Cavalry under Captain DeGress, who had periodically commanded the post during 1870. The captain, three times breveted to colonel during the Civil War, retired December 31, 1870, moved to Austin, Texas, and became a successful businessman. He left this world in 1894 and was buried at Austin.[46]

Col. Ranald S. Mackenzie had been transferred to commanding officer of the 4th U.S. Cavalry in December 1870. Mackenzie became a legend in Texas while commanding that outstanding regiment.

When Major Bliss returned from Fort Clark on January 20, 1871, he brought with him the Headquarters and another company of 25th Infantry. The garrison then contained Companies E and I with Headquarters, 25th Infantry; Company K, 24th Infantry; and Company L, 9th Cavalry. Attached to the post was one company, SNIS, comprising eleven men. Fort Duncan would maintain this strength throughout most of 1871 with an aggregate of seven officers and 242 enlisted.[47]

By May 1871, most of the garrison, including cavalry infantry, was involved in short-term scouting and actively engaged against "Hostile Indians." Nearly 160 officers and men were absent for these activities. The Seminole scouts were in the saddle constantly with different units and on May 1 received a commander at Fort Duncan. Bliss appointed 1st Lt. Thomas Edward Merritt, 24th Infantry, a Civil War veteran, to replace Lieutenant Leggett, who had been appointed post acting assistant adjutant.[48]

Bliss, as all post commanders, responded to written directives of the War Department to adequately describe his station and its needs. For the year 1871, Fort Duncan, Texas, appears as the following:

> . . . Post office is located at the post trader's store, within the limits of the post. Eagle Pass, Maverick County, Texas, a town of one thousand two hundred and fifty inhabitants, is located on the northern boundary of the post, separated by a deep narrow canyon, and connected with the post by a light foot- bridge. Piedras Negras . . . containing two thousand inhabitants, is located immediately opposite the post. *Quarters*—Sufficient for one hundred men, have been repaired and occupied . . . Quarters for three hundred men . . . are being rapidly repaired. Officers' quarters—six sets, built of stone, are repaired and occupied, and others being repaired. Two officers and two companies of infantry are at present occupying tents.
> *Store Houses*—One two-story stone building containing storerooms, and offices occupied by quartermaster and commissary of subsistence. Quartermaster's store-room is in the second story, and is 32 by 27 feet, with office 19 by 27 feet, in north end. Commissary store-room, 51 by 27 feet, on ground floor . . . Magazine—one stone building, 16 by 18 feet . . . one room. Hospital, Guard-House, built of

stone, 60 by 20 feet, with gallery all around, contains one ward 20 by 35 feet, with capacity twenty patients, with dispensary office, store-room, and hospital steward's room. Kitchen to hospital, built of stone, 20 by 10 feet . . . Guard-House—built of stone, 50 by 18 feet, comprising two cells, each 20 by 18 feet . . . Stables—two wooden buildings for Company L, Ninth Cavalry . . .

Supply Depots—The nearest quartermaster and subsistence depots are at San Antonio, Texas, one hundred and fifty-five miles distant. The route of supply is by wagon road, open at all seasons. Supplies are transported . . . as freight, by contract.

Subsistence—six months supply . . . on hand.

Water and Wood—The post is supplied with water from the Rio Grande River, hauled in tanks about one mile and from one cistern in the post. Wood . . . by contract.

Indians—Kickapoos, in Mexico, Comanches and Lipans in Texas, and a small band of Seminole-Negro Indians, who are encamped on the reservation under military control.

Communications—None.

Reservation—The reservation contains eighteen square miles, is owned by John Twohig, of San Antonio, Texas and is leased from him by the Government at $1,560 per year. Description of the country—No arable land. A post garden was undertaken this year, but . . . failure . . . A ferry, owned by a company of citizens at Eagle Pass.

Climate—mild in winter and hot in summer . . .[49]

The post continued rebuilding while at the same time constantly keeping troops in the field after Indians. Throughout 1871, Fort Duncan provided for the security of Maverick, Zavala, and Dimmit counties by General Orders #6, Department of Texas, Col. J. J. Reynolds, commanding.

On July 21, 1871, the post was visited by Colonel Reynolds on his yearly inspection of posts within his department. At this time Reynolds responded to repeated requests from the citizens of Eagle Pass to assist police and rangers in the control, arrest, and confinement of Mexican thieves and bandits.

September 22, 1871, proved to be another tragic and exciting day on the frontier: "A party of Indians made a dash into Eagle Pass and killed two citizens and carried off about forty head of horses." Major Bliss became aware of the incident immediately and ordered Capt. David Schooley in immediate pursuit. This incident had caused such outrage among Eagle Pass residents that several armed and mounted men rode into the post as Schooley and his lieutenant, Patrick Kelleher, born in Ireland and well recognized by his brogue, readied eight men of Company E, 25th Infantry and twenty-seven men of Company L, 9th Cavalry.[50] This provisional detachment of troops was made necessary by the fact other companies were already in the field on different scouts. The command quickly formed and took the trail of the Indians. The outcome, like so many, was reported:

> Headquarters Department of Texas
> (Texas and Louisiana)
> San Antonio, Texas, November 9,
> General Orders
> No. 17
> ...8. Captain D. Schooley, 25th Infantry, with Second Lieutenant P. Kelleher, 25th Infantry, twenty-seven men of Company L, 9th Cavalry, and seventeen citizens, including the well known Indian fighter Manuel Ban, left Fort Duncan September 22, 1871, in pursuit of Indians who were raiding in the vicinity. The trail was found and followed with such energy that before noon of the 22nd the Indians were in sight, near the mouth of Las Moras Creek; but owing to the fact that the Indians were continually mounting fresh horses and dropping the jaded ones, the scout could not force them to a fight, and was barely able to keep them in sight for a distance of forty miles farther, when the Indians succeeded in eluding pursuit.
> The scout recaptured thirteen animals.
> By Command of Colonel J. J. Reynolds:
> H. Clay Woods
> Assistant Adjutant General.[51]

The orders were in "recognition of the energy and good conduct by those who took part . . . against hostile Indians." It is interesting to note there were no SNIS along and as yet, Lieutenant

Bullis was serving with his regiment at Fort McKavett, Texas, northwest of Kerrville. Even more interesting is the fact that the incident was reported in General Sheridan's "Record of Engagements" for 1871 as having occurred near Fort Sill, Indian Territory. Communications broke down somewhere, because the record of events for Fort Duncan go into some detail regarding the episode and certainly the Department of Texas General Orders should preclude any doubt whatsoever.[52]

As the year proceeded to its close, rumblings from across river in Mexico began to be felt at Fort Duncan. The 27th Seminole Negro Indian scout enlisted, and he and his family were welcomed by the others living on the flats adjacent to and downriver from the post. Scouting was a primary function but with little result in capturing the Indians responsible for depredations. Col. Abner Doubleday returned to chair a general court-martial in October 1871, his first visit since 1854. It is assured that he and Major Bliss spent many hours in pleasant reminiscences. The court-martial involved 1st Lt. Archibald Bogle and Asst. Surgeon Alfred C. Girard. On August 27, 1871, Bogle attempted to assassinate Girard by pistol. He missed and was wounded by Girard in self-defense. The court found Bogle guilty and dismissed him from service, but because of his excellent record recommended no sentence to the penitentiary. This judgement was upheld by the presidents.[53]

Desertions averaged four a month with about half caught and tried. A quartermaster clerk was hired at $100 month and a blacksmith at $75 per month. When the SNIS swelled to twenty-seven on September 1, 1871, the post boasted a garrison of nearly 300 men. However, because of the extremely high number of scouts, the aggregate remained low. Scouts were usually seven to twelve days in length and would include seven to fifteen SNIS and normally a doctor. The area most frequented was the Nueces River and La Pendencia and Carrizo Creeks. Those points of reference were heavily patrolled in the three counties aforementioned.

For the safety of the post while most of the troops were in the field, a pair of three-inch field pieces (artillery) were in place. The guns had been brought to Duncan in mid-1869 and represented knowledge that that portion of the frontier was indeed volatile and highly charged with danger.

The Mexican situation deteriorated as political factions favoring the policies of Benito Juarez and Porfirio Diaz tried to sway feelings toward each. Mexican government troops were vital to any success, and the northern Mexican garrison at Piedras Negras would prove pivotal.

The commander of the Mexican garrison was Col. Pedro Advicula Valdes, whom the Indians called "Guinca" (Win-kah). The Americans unable to pronounce Spanish correctly followed the Indians by calling him Colonel Winker or plain Winker. His pacification of the hostiles in northern Coahuila was unprecedented and was never matched, before or since. Entering the Mexican military at nineteen, he sided with Juarez and was instrumental in bringing defeat upon Maximilian's French Regulars. His abilities were not unrewarded. By 1871, "Winker" had risen to full colonel and commanded 250 troops at Piedras Negras.

Mexican sympathies were divided in 1870-71 between Juarez and another hero of the French campaigns named Porfirio Diaz. Popular and ambitious, he "proclaimed" and revolution began anew in the republic. The showdown was between supporters of Juarez and Diaz for control of the government and Mexico—a worthy prize. Each faction appealed to zealots and protectionists alike. Valdes, a self-proclaimed proponent of Juarez, was soon forced to defend himself against a General Falcon, a Diaz follower. Falcon, with an army of 1,300 men, marched on Piedras Negras and demanded surrender of Valdes. Unwilling and never agreeing to capitulate, Winker in December 1871 fortified Piedras Negras and settled down to siege. Other than a few determined attacks by the Falcon troops, the Mexican town, its garrison, and Colonel Valdes continued to hold their own against overwhelming odds.[55]

It is one thing to whip a dead horse in frustration, but to expect life again is folly. Valdes was no fool. Well acquainted with the officers at Fort Duncan, both professionally and socially, Winker knew American intervention was the only recourse to the current deadlock. He directed his men to fire on the U.S. side of the Rio Grande and especially the Fort Duncan area each time Falcon troops attempted to invade Piedras Negras. Of course, Major Bliss, commanding at Duncan, had to relieve a potential deadly threat. During a clandestine meeting, Bliss informed Valdes that further firing into the post or U.S. side of the river would invite retaliatory cannon fire from Fort Duncan.[56] The incident became a cause célèbre with the faroff *New York Herald* headlining with, "The Ultimatum of Bliss the Federal Commander."

Several months dragged by until February 1872. A dark-of-night meeting took place when Valdes, wet, bedraggled and bleeding from the loss of a thumb to musket fire, as well as a shoulder wound, asked Bliss to remove his guards near the river. His intention was to cross his command and escape into the interior to regroup for another day. Bliss informed Winker that he and his men would be held as prisoners of war. Winker tried to cross undetected, was captured, and then held at Fort Duncan. His failed ruse unsupported, Winker told Bliss that he had left a few surprises in Piedras Negras for General Falcon. Soon a fusillade erupted. Dummies, dead horses, and other assorted impediments absorbed the whole of Falcon's attack, and Winker applied himself fully of the special Mexican humor at outsmarting an adversary. Later, Winker joined the Diaz government and resumed his commission as a colonel. Noted Indian fighter and loyalist Winker was characterized by Bliss as "The bravest man I ever saw." [57]

That same February of 1872 forced the Americans to be more vigilant and the garrison prepared for any eventuality. On the 11th, a scout of thirty men including fifteen SNIS was recalled back to post because of "revolution on Mexican side of the Rio Grande."

On February 4, 1872, the Department of Texas received a new and popular commander, Brig. Gen. Christopher Colon Augur. Graduate of the Military Academy in 1839, Augur was an experienced troop commander, leader, and motivator. Three times breveted during the Civil War, he accepted responsibility and determined to end the long-term suffering of citizens in his department. The general was not timid, for he began an immediate realignment of troops. In April, Bliss was reassigned to Fort Concho. Fort Duncan was garrisoned by one company each from the 24th and 25th Infantry and 9th Cavalry. The Seminole Negro Indian Scouts numbered twenty-five. Thus the year was spent in constant scouts to curtail Indian and bandit depredations. [58]

May 20, 1872, Lt. Gustavus Valois with a detachment of the 9th Cavalry from Fort Duncan and eight SNIS surprised a small band of Kickapoo while patrolling La Pendencia Creek. The action brought no casualties or captured animals on either side, but gave notice that the soldiers were very active in their scouts.

The 9th Cavalry with headquarters and four new companies arrived at Fort Clark in April of 1872. Lt. Col. Wesley Merritt commanded but was too few in number and had too much territory to cover. Augur pleaded with Sheridan to bring more cavalry to the border, and the remainder of the 9th was sent from Forts Stockton and Davis.

By August 1872, Merritt had attracted seventeen Seminole Negro Indian Scouts and recruited an additional five.[59] Those men and their families comprised the nucleus for scouts whose relatives were still on active duty into 1914 at Fort Clark.

Smallpox came to Fort Duncan in October 1872. The epidemic, then called "Variola," laid waste to Eagle Pass. The post surgeons insisted on a strict quarantine and the soldiers were better protected. In time the "pox" subsided, and with the other "Three Horsemen" rode on.[60]

On December 2, General Augur relieved the acting post commanders of Capts. Gaines Lawson and David Schooley and Maj. Henry Merriam with Lt. Col. William R. Shafter. It had been three and one-half years since Shafter had briefly stopped at Duncan, and that occasion had resulted in a court of inquiry. However, he was to remain for the next four years and was instrumental in helping to pacify the Indians and lawless elements until civilization brought order to the Rio Grande frontier. Shafter brought a company of his 24th Infantry but relieved it with one at the post, which he sent to Ringgold Barracks at Rio Grande City on December 5.[61]

Fort Duncan began 1873 with its new commander and a garrison made up of two companies of the 24th Infantry, one company of the 9th Cavalry, and one company of SNIS (fourteen). Total aggregate was 193 officers and men until January 14, when an acting assistant surgeon died of apoplexy.

This year would be the beginning of harsh and successful measures against raiding Indians. Too long the suffering of innocents had gone unchallenged. Momentous changes in military thinking were being born. No longer could the federal government ignore the continuous pleas for help. The Kickapoos and Lipans, safe in their Mexican sanctuary, denied all efforts at resettlement on U.S. reservations. The Comanche and Kiowa, with some few southern Cheyennes, depredated with impunity in northern and western

Texas. Uncontrolled by current military and state militia techniques, the border and frontier areas were nightmares to isolated ranchers and village inhabitants. Lieutenant Colonel Merritt, commanding Fort Clark and all military between Fort McIntosh at Laredo and the Pecos River, was unable to visibly alter the chaotic situation. His regiment, the 9th Cavalry, could never be concentrated for mass retaliation, and his responsibilities totally overwhelmed his vastly separated command. The fact his handful of detachments could not cross the international boundary, even in hot pursuit of offenders, reduced his efforts to endless patrols without chance of success.

Besieged by entreaties from Texas, the administration of President U. S. Grant was forced to act. General of the Army William T. Sherman was consulted and ordered to punish those Indians known to be raiding as far north of the Rio Grande as San Antonio and Fredericksburg. Atascosa County had become a veritable cornucopia for marauding Kickapoo.

Sherman directed Gen. Philip Sheridan, commanding the Division of the Missouri, under which the Department of Texas was subordinate, to transfer the 4th Cavalry, commanded by Col. Ranald S. Mackenzie, to Fort Clark. Mackenzie was to be given carte blanche to remedy the "Kickapoo problem" with a quick, decisive, and bold maneuver. This was to be accomplished by whatever means deemed appropriate and without embarrassment to the administration. Mackenzie, the field commander, was given tacit but unwritten approval to attack the Kickapoo near their village in Mexico. Further, he was to be given the luxury of concentrating his full regiment in southwest Texas and using them as cavalry shock troops to disband, break-up, capture, or destroy those Indians guilty of crimes against border Texans.[62]

Activity became feverish as detached companies of the cavalry began marching toward the Rio Grande. Shafter in early April 1873 offered space to Mackenzie for at least two of his companies.

Company M, 4th Cavalry, responding to orders, arrived at Fort Duncan April 8, 1873. Its commander, Capt. William O'Connell, with Lt. Otho Budd marched from Fort Ringgold. 2nd Lt. John L. Bullis, 24th Infantry, was ordered to report to Fort Duncan as acting quartermaster and commissary of subsistence.

Shafter obviously needed this officer in a most important staff position. However, shortly after arrival, Bullis was relieved of his regimental staff assignment and appointed chief of scouts.[63]

That directive authorizing Lieutenant Bullis to command the Seminole Negro Indian Scouts was dated May 1, 1873, in Special Order No. 50, Headquarters, 24th Infantry, Fort Duncan, and signed by Lt. Col. William R. Shafter, commanding regiment and post. The assignment did not place Bullis in command of all SNIS, as some have suggested, but only those at Fort Duncan. Other posts had other officers as chief of scouts, and in 1873 the SNIS were commanded at Fort Clark by the adjutant of the 4th Cavalry, 1st Lt. Leopold O. Parker.[64] For the record, Bullis did move to Fort Clark later and spent the majority of his time with the scouts from that post.

On the night of May 16, 1873, a courier arrived from Fort Clark requesting Bullis and his command for a combat assignment with Colonel Mackenzie and his 4th Cavalry. Within minutes, Bullis had gathered sixteen SNIS with weapons and accouterments and was in the saddle heading toward a rendezvous on Las Moras Creek, twelve miles below Fort Clark. They were attached to an attack column of six companies of the 4th Cavalry, three guides, and eighteen SNIS from Fort Clark. Colonel Mackenzie placed Bullis' command at the head of the column, and they crossed the Rio Grande near Quemado, Texas, at a ford known as Paso de las Piedras Negras a little after 9:00 P.M. on the 17th. Their destination was a small village on the San Rodrigo River called Remolino. It was near here that the Kickapoo, Lipan, and Mescaleros had set up housekeeping in their cane houses called "wickiup."

They were known to guides and citizens for depredating on the frontier, then retreating with their spoils to a sanctuary of ready buyers in Mexico.

The command attacked those Indians May 18, 1873, killing nineteen and capturing fifteen women, twenty-four children, sixty-five horses and Costilietos (cost-e- lee-a-toes), a feeble chief of the Lipans. Blind and infirm, he was unable to escape while the brunt of attack was committed against the Kickapoo. Lariated by Scout Renty Grayson, he was dragged unceremoniously to the other captives.

Devastating to the Kickapoo, that raid into Mexico, unsupported by treaty, convinced the Indians and their Mexican benefac-

tors that the U.S. would no longer tolerate transgressions, no matter where the transgressors might hide.[65]

Curiously, it was not until July 29, 1882, that a protocol between Mexico and Washington, nine years after the Mackenzie
Raid, was signed. That document authorized *regular* troops of both
republics the reciprocal right of crossing the international boundary
when *in hot pursuit of Indians.*

Mackenzie, niggardly in praise of others, wrote highly of support from Fort Duncan. His official report, dated May 23, 1873,
specifically stated: ". . . wish to mention Lieut. Bullis with the
Seminole Scouts who charged under the command of that gallant
officer very well . . . I wish to express my great obligations to Lieut.
Col. Shafter commanding Fort Duncan for his very cordial coopera-
tion and his entire support he has given me throughout." [67]

No sooner had Mackenzie's command returned than he sent
Companies E and M, 4th Cavalry to Fort Duncan. Space requirements contributed heavily to dispersal of troops. Headquarters 4th
Cavalry remained at Fort Clark, but several elements were detached
to small unit camps for better control of exigencies.

Shafter was responsible for security in his area, and with
rumor of Kickapoo and Mexican retaliation for Mackenzie's raid
sent the cavalry to river camps to scout. One such cantonment was
called Camp Shafter and was established by Lieutenant Thurston
and Company E on May 28, 1873. Its location was twenty-five
miles southwest of Fort Duncan on Comanche Creek in Dimmit
County.[68]

This property is now part of the Ewing Halsell Foundation
and known as Las Farias Ranch. Through the kindness of Gilbert
Denman, chairman, and Helen Campbell of the foundation's Board
of Directors, the author was allowed access to the ranch. Tito
Ritchie, who lives on the ranch, acted as guide most of a day trying
to pinpoint Camp Shafter. Unfortunately, Comanche Creek was
dammed many years ago, creating a twelve-acre lake and forever
changing the course of the creek in its destination to the Rio
Grande. That camp, like many others, has been lost to historians—
not by malice but by private ranch management.

Camp Shafter served as many as two companies at a time and
provided a semi-permanent cantonment for scouts all along the Rio
Grande. Camp San Pedro Springs was another well used canton-

ment and provided a base of operations for Indian scouting expeditions for several years. That area also lies hidden within private ranchlands.

Fort Duncan paid host to the Border Claims commissioners from April 6, 1873, until they left to meet with Mackenzie, Sheridan, Stanton, et al. at Fort Clark on April 12. The following day, Secretary of War Stanton and Lt. Gen. Philip Sheridan arrived at the post for inspection. They stayed the day and night before leaving for Fort McIntosh on April 14.

Throughout the rest of 1873, Duncan remained home for Companies D and K, 24th Infantry and E and M, 4th Cavalry. However, scouting activity was furious, and the troops' use of Fort Duncan was confined to mail pick-up and obtaining rations and forage.

Still prepared for retaliatory action after Mackenzie's Mexican raid, the post was visited by Colonel Mackenzie and a detachment of Company K, 4th Cavalry, who joined the garrison temporarily. While the cavalry were stationed at small camps and ranches nearby they remained primarily under the direction of Colonel Mackenzie. 2nd Lt. John L. Bullis and his SNIS, although part of the Fort Duncan garrison, were used as couriers between the troops at Camp Shafter and Mackenzie's Headquarters at Fort Clark.[69]

On October 14, 1873, reliable information reached Shafter that Governor Pedro Cepeda of Coahuila and several armed men from Mexico had crossed the Rio Grande near the cavalry Camp Shafter. Immediately he ordered Lieutenant Thurston with forty men to intercept and capture Cepeda. The lieutenant's patrol failed to find any trace of the Mexicans and returned to their camp on the 17th after marching 110 miles.

Bullis was ordered out with his command of scouts on October 28, under Special Order #133, Fort Duncan. As the year wound down, those companies separated from the post were called in by Shafter and arrived October 31. Company K, 24th Infantry was transferred elsewhere by Special Order #171, Department of Texas, and left Fort Duncan October 5. The garrison in December consisted of two companies of the 24th and 25th Infantry and two companies of the 4th Cavalry temporarily commanded by Maj. A. L. Latimer, 4th Cavalry.[71]

Mackenzie's border crossing, without written orders, was

cause for perfunctory challenge from the Mexican government, but Sheridan and his military superiors sustained him.[72] The people of Texas were ecstatic and breathed a collective sigh of relief as Indian depredations were reduced to a trickle. The 13th Legislature, sitting in Austin by joint resolution, praised Mackenzie's efforts by issuing ". . . the Grateful Thanks of the people of the State . . . due to General Mackenzie and the troops under his command, for their prompt action and gallant conduct in inflicting well merited punishment upon these scourges of our frontier." The fact that "Grateful Thanks" had been languishing in different committees for over a year for Mackenzie's services in *northwest* Texas does not lessen its importance. Remarkably, at no time before or since had similar resolution by any legislature for a specific engagement ever been written.[73]

In his official report of the incident Mackenzie singled out several officers for special mention, authorized no brevets, and remarkably requested medals of honor for two of the enlisted personnel wounded during the action. Their names were Pvts. William Pair and Peter Corrigan, both of Company I. Higher headquarters did not endorse this recommendation, and no awards were made.

The year 1874 proved highly interesting, and Fort Duncan was a major post in the successes enjoyed that year by U.S. troops.

January began as 1873 had ended. Lieutenant Colonel Shafter managed a brief leave and Major Latimer still commanded the post. The garrison consisted of two companies of 24th Infantry and two of 4th Cavalry with a detachment of six SNIS for a total aggregate of 119 men and officers.

One of those infrequent military transfers between officers of different branches of service took place that early January. Lt. George Alva Thurston, 4th Cavalry since 1867, made a lateral change to the 3rd Artillery and was replaced in the cavalry by 1st Lt. Charles Michael Callahan, 3rd Artillery, on January 13, 1874. Callahan was promoted to captain in 1879; Thurston did not receive his double silver bars until 1889. One wonders why the transfer occurred.[74] Had Thurston had enough of frontier Texas or horse soldiering? Had Callahan, possibly tired of caisson grapeshot, longed for immediate action in the cavalry? It remains one of the many historical inconsistencies and frustrations that forever baffle writer and reader alike.

In February, normally chilly in South Texas, Lt. Otho Budd and Company M, 4th Cavalry with Lieutenant Bullis and his command of SNIS reported to Colonel Mackenzie at Fort Clark for scouting duty. Unwilling to remain idle or accept accolades for duty performed, the frontier military of the Department of Texas and Rio Grande District in particular maintained active patrolling. Because of the severity of scouting and constant movement, two companies of the 4th Cavalry traded places every other month between Forts Duncan and Clark.

In May of 1874, Gen. C. C. Augur, Department of Texas commander, and staff arrived at the post. They were on their way to Fort Clark to confer with Colonel Mackenzie regarding Sheridan's plan for pursuing the Southern Plains Indians known to be somewhere in the panhandle of Texas. The general spent the night and leaving next morning was escorted by Capt. Peter Boehm, E Company, 4th Cavalry. Boehm, an MOH (Medal of Honor) recipient from the Civil War, left the commander's entourage at Clark and went on to camp at the mouth of Las Moras Creek and the Rio Grande. This area, now on private land and known as Las Moras Ranch, is historically significant and contains a building first built in 1862. Although Boehm in 1874 was probably the first military to maintain a cantonment there, Indians had used the area for many years, and burial remains were found as late as 1988.[75]

Planning was extensive for the upcoming campaign called the Red River War. Mackenzie started west with part of his command toward a rendezvous northwest of Fort Concho. Designated the Southern Column, it was one of five commands in the field during the late summer, fall, and winter of 1874. Their destination was the High Plains of Texas, where they hoped to surround and force surrender of those Comanche, Kiowa, and southern Cheyenne who were felt to be concentrated there.

Company K, 4th Cavalry and a detachment of SNIS left Fort Duncan August 3, 1874, to join the Southern Column in the field. The post was then further reduced to Company D, 24th Infantry and Company A, 25th Infantry when the Field Staff and Band, 24th Infantry was ordered to Fort Brown per Special Order 148, Department of Texas on October 15. Their departure left Capt. John French, 25th Infantry, commanding his company and the post through year's end. The officers present December 31 included

French, C. C. Gray, surgeon, Capt. Charles N.W. Cunningham, commanding Company D, 24th Infantry, and the remaining Seminole Negro Indian Scouts. 1st Lt. Andrew Geddes continued as post adjutant and second in command under French.[76]

During the last month of 1874 and close to Christmas, an incident occurred involving the SNIS at Fort Duncan. The town adjacent, Eagle Pass, was a haven for border toughs and badmen. One such was "King" Fisher, whose boast of killing a man for every year of his life, "not counting Mexicans," produced fear in the inhabitants. His gang habitually ran roughshod over the community. While off-duty, several scouts were enjoying the pleasures of an infamous dive known as the Blue Goose Saloon that December. Fisher and his gang, unused to confrontation, particularly by black men, attempted to intimidate the scouts, but they did not scare easily. Veterans of several combats, the scouts pulled their sidearms and "let the devil take the hindermost." Guns fired, and when the smoke cleared, a scout lay badly wounded. The army, unwilling to demand satisfaction, effectively handled the problem by transferring most of the scouts to Fort Clark—including Lieutenant Bullis. Fisher had his head creased by a scout's bullet, but Cpl. George Washington, a nephew of the chief of the Seminole Negro Indians, died May 9, 1875, from his wound.[77]

Although King Fisher and his outlaw gang remained in Eagle Pass after the shootout, they did not tempt fate again by bullying soldiers.

Lieutenant Colonel Shafter was ordered to head an infantry equipment board at Fort Leavenworth and dutifully left Fort Duncan in late May 1874. He did not return until February 1875, when the new department commander, Gen. E.O.C. Ord, ordered him to sweep the plains, known as Llano Estacado, of any hostiles not already driven in by Mackenzie et al. during the Red River Campaign of 1874-75. That scout saw Shafter leaving the post in late May 1875 to command nearly 450 troops of the 10th Cavalry and 24th and 25th Infantry. His successful examination of West Texas and subsequent report was of inestimable value to later army and civilians traveling throughout the now known and mapped region.[78]

Companies E and K, 4th Cavalry transferred with their regiment in January 1875 to Fort Sill, Indian Territory. The Fort Duncan garrison consisted of Company D, 24th Infantry and Company A,

25th Infantry, with the one company of SNIS (eleven men), for an aggregate total of 104. Thus began another eventful year for the post.

No sooner had Shafter returned in February than he had troops scouting in the field. The Rio Grande area, particularly, received much attention. Indian scares were daily among the citizens, and every effort was made to keep the hostiles from the settlements.

On March 16 the stage from San Antonio was attacked by Indians just nineteen miles from Fort Duncan. 1st Lt. Andrew Geddes, 25th Infantry, with one corporal from Company D, 24th Infantry and fourteen SNIS, left the post in hot pursuit. The men returned, exhausted, on March 18, having traveled 100 miles. They reported no Indians seen. Unfortunately, that was usually the case, but rapid chase disallowed the hostiles becoming too troublesome. Fort Duncan remained the rock of the Rio Grande defense line, and its presence was incalculable in saving lives and property.

On May 26, 1875, Capt. Charles Parker, 1st Lt. Gustavus Valois, and 2nd Lt. B. S. Humphrey arrived with Company K, 9th Cavalry bringing the garrison to a strength of 178 men.[79] On June 10, Colonel Shafter took the two infantry companies and Seminole Negro Indian Scouts, who were then commanded by 2nd Lt. Edgar Swazie Beacom of the 24th Infantry, and headed west.

Company H, 10th Infantry arrived in June to replace the infantry then on scout with Shafter in West Texas. Shafter and his command did not return to the post until December 21, 1875, having been gone five months and marched 2,000 miles.[80] With the return of Companies D and F, 24th Infantry, the company of 10th Infantry transferred to Fort Clark the day after Christmas.

1st Lt. Alfred Collins Markley was appointed chief of the SNIS at Fort Duncan at year's end.

The new assistant surgeon at the post, Donald Jackson, had arrived in April and had been the medical officer with Col. Ranald S. Mackenzie when the raid into Mexico took place in May 1873. Dr. Jackson, then acting assistant surgeon, had been pointedly commended by Mackenzie for that action and his care of the wounded from the engagement with Kickapoo and Lipan Indians near the village of Remolino, Mexico.[81]

Circular No. 8, "Hygiene of the United States Army, with Descriptions of Military Posts, War Department, 1875" and written by Assistant Surgeon William R. Steinmetz, U.S. Army, gives in fascinating detail the condition of Fort Duncan in 1875.

The stables, situated at the northeast corner of the post, are three in number, two for cavalry horses, and one for the quartermaster's animals. The latter was totally demolished on the 23rd of May, 1873, by a tornado which passed over this section of the country, and its reerection has not yet been completed. One of the cavalry stables was also injured at the same time but has since been repaired and is in use again.

The post library consists of one hundred and seventy volumes of miscellaneous books, which are kept in two hospital tents situated on the parade ground a short distance southeast of the hospital, and used as library and reading room. The latter is open to the garrison from guard-mount until tattoo. Several daily and weekly papers are received. There are also two literary societies at the post, composed of members of the two cavalry companies.

The hospital has no bath or wash rooms, lavatories or urinals. The drainage of the hospital grounds, as also of the entire camp, is natural and sufficient. There is no sewerage.

The main water supply is the Rio Grande river, from which water is hauled in a tank and distributed around the camp. The water is quite sweet and good in winter, but during the summer months becomes very muddy. It can be easily made clear by means of alum, sliced almonds, or other kernels containing hydrocyanic acid, which rapidly precipitate the impurities to the bottom of the barrels. There are also four cisterns, three in rear of the company barracks, and one on the officers' line. Owing to the comparatively great amount of rain which fell during the year (1873) these cisterns have been well supplied with water.

There are no regular arrangements in regard to bathing except for the prisoners, who are required to bathe in the river every Sunday morning when the weather permits.

Owing to the necessity of constant irrigation, it is very difficult to have a post garden; several attempts were made at different times to raise some vegetables in the bottom land in rear of the barracks, without avail. The garrison is, however, well supplied with fresh vegetables and fruits brought from Mexico, and sold at reasonable prices.

Two mails per week are received from San Antonio, Texas, nearest city of any size; from there nearly all supplies received. It requires from two to three days for a mail to reach department headquarters, and from ten to twelve days to reach Washington, D.C.

The population of Eagle Pass, the adjoining town, amounts to about 1,500 inhabitants, consisting of Americans, Germans, and principally Mexicans. Their chief occupation is mercantile business and stock-raising. The late epidemic of smallpox in the winter of 1872 and 1873 decimated the population of both Eagle Pass and the Mexican town which lies on the right bank of the river directly opposite the post, called Piedras Negras (Black Rocks), to such an extent that even the Mexicans were thereby frightened, although they believe that variola is a disease which everyone ought to have once in his life. Both towns were built since the establishment of the post of Fort Duncan.

The above description tells of the post in 1875. It was garrisoned by Headquarters and two battalions of the 3rd U.S. Infantry, and temporary buildings were erected. The post covered an important crossing of the Rio Grande, and it guarded the caravans trading with Mexico both from hostile Indians and others. In 1872 it covered eighteen square miles, and eighty Seminole Negro Indians lived there and furnished scouts for American punitive expeditions against the Lipans, Kickapoos, Comanches and Apaches, under Lt. John L. Bullis and others.[82]

By year's end Shafter had returned from his arduous West Texas scout, and the strength of the post stood at 12 officers and 164 enlisted men. Fort Duncan began 1876 as it ended, but large garrisons were a thing of the past. Although the fort required eight to ten civilian employees (clerk at $75 per month, blacksmith and wheelwright at $60 each monthly, and six teamsters at $30 each monthly), its usefulness was becoming short-lived.

General Ord had further plans for his energetic commander at Fort Duncan. He decided on an early spring campaign, and Shafter met twice with Ord at San Antonio in early 1876 to plan details. General Ord's daughter was married to Mexican General Trevino in San Antonio and sealed good will between those countries.

Since Bullis and most of the SNIS had moved to Fort Clark, only a handful of these scouts remained at Fort Duncan. It is of some interest that after the attack on April 25, 1875, by Bullis and three SNIS on a group of Indians near the Pecos River, the heroism of his scouts was rewarded by three Medals of Honor. Pompey Factor, one of these scouts, received his medal at Fort Duncan on March 15, 1876. The two other scouts, John Ward and Issac Payne,

were stationed at Fort Clark, as was Bullis. Lieutenant Colonel
Shafter presented the medal to Factor, who signed a receipt with his
mark (X).

After Shafter returned from his West Texas scout in December
1875, he appointed 1st Lt. Alfred Collins Markley, 24th Infantry, as
chief of scouts at Fort Duncan.[83]

By April 1876, General Ord and Lieutenant Colonel Shafter
had finalized their plans for a spring roundup of hostiles and bandits. Company F, 24th Infantry was ordered to establish a garrison
at Camp Hudson on the Devils River. Company H, 10th Infantry
replaced Company D, 24th Infantry, which transferred to Fort
Clark.

Lieutenant Colonel Shafter then left Fort Duncan and moved
headquarters to Camp Hudson, where he commanded the spring
summer campaign. This West Texas scout included much arduous
service, and not until October 1876 did Shafter feel satisfied with
his efforts and return to Fort Duncan.[84]

During his absence, Capt. Charles A. Hartwell, 8th Cavalry,
commanded the post. A distinguished Civil War veteran who rose
to brevet brigadier general of Volunteers by war's end, he died prematurely on October 3, 1876, at Castroville, Texas, while en route
to San Antonio.

Shafter now prevailed upon the department commander for
more command responsibility, and Ord, ever appreciative of this officer's efforts, especially the last two years in West Texas, acceded.
Within his department General Ord initiated the District of the
Nueces and appointed Shafter to command. Accordingly, he shifted
the staff and band, 24th Infantry, and Shafter to Fort Clark.

By December 1876, Lieutenant Colonel Shafter with his headquarters and command, now occupied the more congenial post on
the Las Moras.[85] Shafter further ordered all remaining SNIS to
Clark, and by January 1877 Fort Duncan was without those scouts
whom Major Bliss and Captain Perry had originally persuaded to
serve in 1870.

Maj. George Wheeler Schofield, 10th Cavalry, assumed command of Fort Duncan and would remain from January 17, 1877,
until February 11, 1878. It remained a three-company post with one
cavalry and two infantry. The cavalry was kept constantly in the
field scouting for Indians and cattle thieves, the latter being both

Indian and white. Although the post was a major factor in the pacification of hostiles and bandits, other areas wanted and demanded a military garrison. Fort Duncan, long used to secondary status, now became questionable for existence. The pueblo of San Felipe (Del Rio, Texas), with great public relations, began exerting pressure on General Ord at San Antonio for a post for their community. An offer of 400 acres to be deeded to the U.S. government with 1,076 acres free use was presented by the citizens of San Felipe Del Rio to the War Department. General Ord in his recommendation stated "I propose . . . to gradually break up Fort Duncan . . . to build good quarters at San Felipe . . . San Felipe is a much healthier place . . . is nearer the route usually taken by raiders. It can be maintained at much less expense . . . is not . . . where it can be overlooked by the Mexicans . . . and any movement of the troops discovered and opposed."

Although no authority was given for erection of a permanent post, a deed from the San Felipe Agricultural Manufacturing and Irrigation Company was presented to the United States for "a military garrison" on September 28, 1877.[86] As a result of this largess, one company of the 10th Cavalry was ordered to San Felipe as its first garrison. Fort Duncan escaped the hatchet once again.[87]

Not mentioned during the decade of the '70s were the invaluable civilian guides used by Mackenzie, Shafter, et al. Forts Duncan and Clark used extensively the services of scouts Green Vann and Abram Garcia. Intelligent and superior trackers, they were recognized by the army as an integral part of the scouting process. Both risked their lives time and again, while participating individually and collectively with the SNIS to rid Eagle Pass and Brackettville of undesirables.[88]

Garcia pursued an Indian known to have murdered some civilians near Eagle Pass across the Rio Grande. Several days later, Garcia deposited the dead body of the Indian and his possessions on the public square in Eagle Pass as a reminder to those inclined to lawlessness of serious consequences.[89]

Vann was instrumental as both spy and tracker for Mackenzie's raid against Kickapoo in 1873. Later he became a well-known rancher and sheriff in Maverick County. The Rio Grande border area owes much to men such as Vann and Garcia.

Throughout 1877, the garrison at Fort Duncan stayed aggres-

sive in their pursuit of miscreants. Overshadowed by the almost in-
human efforts of Lieutenant Bullis and his command of SNIS from
Fort Clark as they crossed and recrossed the Rio Grande, the post
garrison proved a deterrent to many hostile intentions. On
November 18, 1877, two Mexican sheepherders at the Sauz Ranch
(between Duncan and Laredo) were murdered by Indians. Troops
from Fort Duncan chased them almost to Laredo, Texas, before the
Indians crossed into Mexico and the cavalry was forced to abandon
chase.

In April 1877 word reached General Ord that two Mexican
men, Julian Kongina and Pedro Rodriguez, U.S. Army guides, were
being held in Piedras Negras against their will. The *alcalde* of
Piedras Negras on request to release the men stated he would be
obliged to arrest anyone guiding American troops across the Rio
Grande.

Shafter, on orders from Ord, marched immediately to Fort
Duncan and early on April 3, 1877, crossed the big river with three
companies of the 10th Cavalry, while sending Major Schofield with
two companies of the 24th Infantry wading across directly in front
of the Mexican village. The combined force occupied the town
plaza, but their efforts were in vain. Both men had been taken from
the jail and sent further south. The Shafter raid returned to the U.S.
side with little but a well-coordinated cavalry-infantry exercise to
critique.[90]

June 1, 1877, became a landmark date in governmental action.
Shafter's superiors and the War Department had requested numerous times permission to cross into Mexico to punish offenders. No
treaty existed between Washington and Mexico allowing formal intrusion of the other's sovereignty; however, Secretary of War
George McCrary authorized General Sherman to inform his troops
on the border, ". . . when in pursuit of a band of marauders and
when . . . in sight or upon a fresh trail, . . . follow them across the
Rio Grande, and to overtake and punish them, . . . and recover
stolen property." This policy was already in use by both Shafter and
Bullis but was not legitimized.[91] Unfortunately, U.S. government
vacillation, Mexican criticism, and the Quaker Peace Policy would
countermand this permission several times before final treaty protocol was accepted in 1882.

The end of 1877 closed a staggering number of scouts and relentless chases. Probably for any one year, 1877 saw the most activity at Fort Duncan. Again, the old post was subject to closing with a new replacement at San Felipe del Rio. Again, fortuitous circumstances prevented its closure. Congressional action regarding the military was minimal. Appropriations that year were not released until November, thus eliminating new posts along the border.[92]

The never-ceasing demands by increasing numbers of citizens besieged government at all levels for better protection. Shafter, from his headquarters now at Fort Clark, kept his troops in the field with amazing regularity. But the winds of change swept 1878 into a new era with replacement, a new regiment, and a new commander of the District of the Nueces.

Loud and demanding, the congressional delegation from Texas was a powerful element. Unwilling to accept further criticism for lack of protection from their constituents, mainly the border area, they dangled military purse strings before General Sherman.

Desirous of an immediate solution, the delegation implied more military spending if Col. Ranald S. Mackenzie would assume his old command at Fort Clark with his crack 4th Cavalry Regiment. Supposedly, their almost canonized reputation in Texas would provide the impetus to forever relieve border Texas of hostiles and badmen.

Shafter and Mackenzie were old friends and mutually respectful of the other's abilities. No doubt some amount of disappointment rankled Shafter, particularly since the department he commanded had been created for him and his plans.

Mackenzie and his regiment left Fort Sill, I.T., and once again marched for the border and the Rio Grande. It had been four years since he left Fort Clark to command the Southern Column during the Red River War. Subsequent campaigns included the Dull Knife Battle in Wyoming to culminate the 1876 Plains Indian campaigns and confrontations throughout the Indian Territory, all considered successful. Little wonder that Mackenzie's magical reputation inspired the greatest of confidence as a professional soldier.

Throughout 1877 Fort Duncan remained a three-company post including two infantry and one cavalry. The mounted arm remained busy chasing both Indian and Mexican cattle thieves. On November 18, 1877, a Mexican sheepherder was killed on the Sauz Ranch, and the cavalry gave chase to Indians who perpetrated the

crime. However, as so many times before, the troops from Fort
Duncan would follow a hot trail until near Laredo, Texas, where the
murderers slipped across the Rio Grande and were lost in the vast-
ness of Mexico.[93]

By February of 1878, Lieutenant Colonel Shafter had vacated
his headquarters at Fort Clark and his command of the District of
Nueces. He returned to Fort Duncan and resumed command of
that post.

Fort Duncan enlarged in strength by March 1878 to include
three companies of Shafter's 24th Infantry, one company of the
25th Infantry, one company of 4th Cavalry, and one company of
10th Cavalry. Although the mounted troops were normally in the
field, the post was severely strained to accommodate all hands.[94]

During this time and for many years previous, an odd assortment of ruffians, goons, and misguided men rallied to the cause
generally known as filibusters. These groups usually congregated
near the border in order to splash across and capture blacks who
had run away from slavery in the United States. Their activities
were illegal, and measures to control the miscreants included the
U.S. military.

In April 1878 a large band of filibusters headed toward Laredo.
Shafter ordered Lieutenant Bullis and twenty-five men of the cavalry to arrest and disperse these individuals. After confronting the
mob the cavalry swept the area, capturing two, and turned them
over to authorities in Laredo. This action was only one of the duties U.S. troops on the frontier considered routine and which kept
the flag constantly in motion to discourage lawlessness as well as
Indian depredations.[95]

By now Colonel Mackenzie had completed his plans for a
major campaign to reenter Mexico where he had been so successful
in 1873. Troops began to assemble at or near Fort Clark for a large
command to take the field against marauding Indians whose refuge
was in Mexico. This sanctuary prohibited punishment until Colonel
Mackenzie, with six companies of his veteran 4th Cavalry and the
intrepid Seminole Negro Indian Scouts, crossed the border and ren-
dered severe punishment on a band of Kickapoo, Lipans, and
Mescalero Apaches.[96]

Unfortunately, the spoils of raids and the natural desires of re-
calcitrant Indians again spread mayhem across the middle border

region. Colonel Mackenzie and his crack troops were brought to Fort Clark to deny the enemy once and for all his forays into Texas.

Fort Duncan supported this campaign by sending Companies A and B, 24th Infantry and Company E, 4th Cavalry to join the expedition on June 10, 1878. They returned to post June 23 after a march of 136 miles, mostly in Mexico. The campaign was significant only because it precipitated a confrontation between Colonel Mackenzie and a Mexican officer commanding troops which threatened to bar the way for Mackenzie. Needless to say, the colonel did not back down, and the troops under the American flag continued without further interference.[97]

Companies G and K, 10th Infantry arrived June 28, 1878, to relieve the void left by the Mackenzie expedition. Those units were rapidly assimilated throughout the region, some to Fort Clark and others to the field.

Scouting for hostiles remained continuous for the balance of 1878 while Duncan remained a three-company garrison. By February 1878, hostiles, bandits, and filibusters were very troublesome. Since November 18, 1877, when the cavalry had rapidly marched to Sauz Ranch in response to the Indian murders of two sheepherders, Fort Duncan troops lived in the field. That ranch, midway between Duncan and Laredo, presented a trail by the Indians which led to a well-used crossing of the Rio Grande.

By now the company of the 4th Cavalry were regular visitors to the Laredo area and in April 1878 captured two filibusters and turned them over to authorities at that Rio Grande township. Lieutenant Bullis and twenty-five of his company continued their hard riding in pursuit of all perpetrators.

Colonel Mackenzie, having completed his expedition, departed Fort Clark in December 1878 for Washington, D.C. on detached service. Shafter moved over to Clark to assume the command of that post and the District of the Nueces.

The new year of 1879 began at Fort Duncan with two companies of 24th Infantry and one company of 4th Cavalry ably commanded by Captain Crandal of the former regiment.

By March, Lieutenant Colonel Shafter, feeling lonesome for his own, ordered the field, staff, and band of the 24th Infantry to change posts with their 4th Cavalry counterparts. This was completed by March 12 and 13. Fort Duncan appointed a new post adjutant in 1st Lt. Joseph Dorst, 4th Cavalry.[98] Capt. Charles Hood, 24th Infantry, assumed command of Fort Duncan in May of 1879.

After long years of arduous service and twelve years as a lieutenant colonel, Shafter finally received his silver eagles. No other lieutenant colonel had given more or been more successful in a post or field command. Shafter deserved that promotion and received many congratulatory messages from both senior and junior officers. He was granted a few months' leave and then ordered to join his new regiment as its commanding officer.

That regiment was the 1st Infantry, and for the first time in sixteen years Shafter left his beloved black soldiers. The 1st was a regiment of excellent reputation, but some regret must have piqued the former commander who had trained and led his black regiments into sound combat units.[99]

On July 28, 1879, Lt. Col. John B. Yard assumed Shafter's rank and position in the 24th Infantry and as commander of Fort Duncan.

The frontier kept expanding with continuous movement by settlers into western Texas. Two forts supporting this movement and its protection were Davis and Stockton. However, they were located too far north for the lower road and the route of the railroad then expanding westward from San Antonio. Necessity demanded a military presence, and a post was authorized by the District of the Pecos and located near Marathon, Texas. The site chosen was a point four miles south of town near the Rainbow Cliffs (slate rock that caused many hues of color as sunlight touched the rocks) and Maravillas Creek, whose springs offered cool, fresh water in abundance. The new post was designated Camp Pena Colorado (literally "red rock"), and a new road by soldier labor began between Fort Clark and the new station.[100]

As a result of this decision, road builders began from the new post east and the eastern end began at the Pecos River by Company B, 24th Infantry that left Fort Duncan to begin the onerous duty in October 1879. Their place was immediately taken by Company F, 2nd Artillery, who marched over from Fort Clark.[101]

By the last quarter of 1879, Duncan had grown to include Companies A, B and F, 24th Infantry; Company E, 4th Cavalry; Company B, 8th Cavalry; and Company F, 2nd Artillery. All in all, it was a strong post of 231 men and officers with various horses and mules.[102]

Company E, 4th Cavalry had served off and on at Duncan since April 1873. It was finally relieved, and by January 1880 the post was further reduced by artillery as well, leaving 214 men and officers.

Special Orders #107, Department of Texas, sent Company B, 24th Infantry to San Felipe (Del Rio), Texas to continue road building toward Pena Colorado. February 1880 removed Company A, 24th Infantry to the Pecos River for road building.[103]

At this time Indians were reported causing havoc on hapless Mexicans just south of the Rio Grande. Orders sent a detachment of 8th Cavalry and mounted 24th Infantry to El Jardin, upriver from Eagle Pass, when a band of fifty hostiles reached within eight miles of the border. Alarms reverberated on both sides of the international boundary when this group of Indians killed thirteen Mexicans in a frenzy of depredations. Although the Duncan detachment did not engage this hostile group, it had scouted 130 miles to prevent those Indians from crossing the Rio Grande and molesting U.S. inhabitants.[104]

As the new road was almost finished west, the weary 24th Infantry was transferred with its staff and band to Camp San Felipe and awaited orders moving them to Fort Davis. This movement required replacement at Duncan, and on April 29, 1880, Company F, 20th Infantry and Company A, 8th Cavalry now made up a garrison of eighty-eight men and officers.

On December 10, 1880, Brig. Gen. E.O.C. Ord was transferred from his headquarters at San Antonio and replaced by Col. D. S. Stanley as commanding officer, Department of Texas.

Now began the final solution to the Indian problem. Certainly such a statement sounds cruel and unjust. However, frontier Texas determined to survive, and American policy toward the Indian and bandits (Anglo or Mexican) was military control. To debate or suggest alternative solutions is futile. Fort Duncan existed to maintain peace and order on the Rio Grande frontier.

January 1881 began a new year with new troops. Company C and the Band of the 8th Cavalry joined Company F, 20th Infantry to garrison Fort Duncan. An aggregate of nine officers and 96 enlisted were under the post commander, Lt. Col. A. J. Dallas, 22nd

Infantry. This station now enjoyed several amenities. As a result, civilian employees were deemed necessary. They included one forage master at $100 per month, one blacksmith at $60 per month, one wheelwright at $60, and seven teamsters at $25 each per month.

Companies B and C, 22nd Infantry, marched 169 miles from Fort McKavett, Texas and arrived on January 21, 1881. They replaced Company F, 20th Infantry, which transferred to Fort Ringgold at Rio Grande City. With B Company, 22nd Infantry was the son of the previous department commander, 2nd Lt. E.O.C. Ord, Jr.[105]

The early part of 1881 brought tragedy. Capt. George W. Chilson, 8th Cavalry, committed suicide at 5:00 A.M., January 18, 1881, in a condition recorded as "a fit of insanity." The month also brought back a former department commander, Brig. Gen. C. C. Augur to relieve Colonel Stanley at San Antonio. General Augur had been privy to the momentous expedition in 1873 of Col. R. S. Mackenzie and his now famous raid into Mexico against the Kickapoo.[107]

Although the scouting was relentless, less and less became the need for pursuing or apprehending renegades of any ethnicity. Fort records indicate for the first time that the period between January 10 and December 10, 1881, was without a single engagement or capture of Indians or felons.[108]

The year 1882 blustered into Eagle Pass and whipped the national flag with gusting winds. Still a three-company post, Fort Duncan was home to Company H, 8th Cavalry (the cavalry companies alternating between Clark and Duncan for two to three months at each post), and Companies D and F, 22nd Infantry. Total aggregate strength was eight officers, 135 enlisted, two field pieces, and one Gatling gun. This being the first time the records record a Gatling at Fort Duncan.[109]

A protocol was finally signed between Washington and Mexico to eliminate a long-standing dispute. The 61st Congress in its second session, July 29, 1882, affirmed the "Protocol of an Agreement Concerning Pursuit of Indians Across the Border." Finally, nine years after the daring and successful raid by Gen. Ranald S. Mackenzie to Remolino, Mexico, to punish the Kickapoo and Lipans, both republics granted reciprocal rights of regular troops to cross the international boundary. The only criteria required that troops must be in "hot pursuit."[110]

This situation, so desperately needed previously, was by now moot. Little or no activity existed anymore between hostiles, bandits, and U.S. soldiers. The cavalryman, as Frederic Remington described "one who rode a government horse," was rapidly becoming obsolete. The frontier had long since moved westward and sympathy for the soldier was declining. Eagle Pass began to enjoy regular mail service during 1882.

Approaching year's end, relief of the 22nd Infantry was accomplished when D Company, 19th Infantry arrived on station. A new commanding officer got off the ship at Galveston and, unlike most of his predecessors, proceeded by rail rather than horse to Fort Duncan. He was Lt. Col. Tasker R. Bliss, 19th Infantry. Bliss, a strong staff man, was sent to evaluate further need and obtain command experience. Though long in the army and a graduate of the Military Academy, he had no previous field commands during his service.[111] The post now contained the above with H Company, 8th Cavalry, and the garrison was now seventy-seven officers and enlisted men. In May 1883, Company L, 8th Cavalry rode over from Clark and replaced Company H. Along with two companies of the 19th Infantry the post of Fort Duncan awaited the inevitable dissolution of so much history. Apparently the necessity of showing the flag by a fort full of armed regular soldiers had now become an expensive luxury.

Special Orders No. 98, Department of Texas, were issued by the chief of staff at Fort Sam Houston, Texas. The final abandonment of Fort Duncan, Texas, was ordered to take place August 31, 1883. Troop L, 8th Cavalry and Companies D and F, 19th Infantry, marched in review at the old parade ground while the bugler sounded the call for lowering the colors. No more would Fort Duncan serve the border and its inhabitants. Its usefulness had been outlived, its buildings left to vandalism, decay, and theft. The flagpole, unguarded and naked of the national symbol, was a silent sentinel until it too vanished.

Painting of Fort Duncan, circa 1870s.

—Fort Duncan Museum

Cavalry training mission returning to Camp Eagle Pass, 1916.

—National Archives

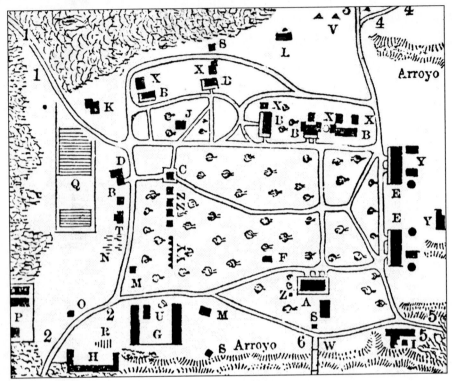

Fort Duncan in 1875.
—Fort Duncan Museum

Small boats called "chalupas" used as ferries across Rio Grande.
—Francisco Barrientos Collection

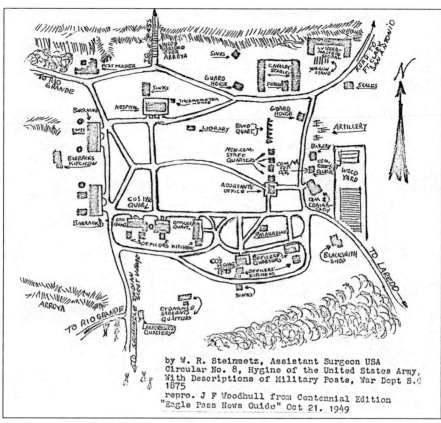

by W. R. Steinmetz, Assistant Surgeon USA
Circular No. 8, Hygine of the United States Army,
With Descriptions of Military Posts, War Dept S.C
1875
repro. J F Woodhull from Centennial Edition
"Eagle Pass News Guide" Oct 21. 1949

*Fort Duncan in 1875, as drawn by Asst. Surgeon W. R. Steinmetz
during an inspection of the post.*

—War Department, U.S. Army, 1875

*Green Vann, aka Manuel Ban.,
Indian fighter and scout.*

—Fort Duncan Museum and
the Paniagua family

*Capt. Ranald S. Mackenzie,
circa 1870.*

—National Archives

Capt. Wintz Miller, 4th Cavalry, circa 1886.
Served at Fort Duncan.

—National Archives
#111-sc-87412

1st Lt. John Lapham Bullis, 24th Infantry,
circa 1874.
—Fort Davis National
Historic Service #AC-47

Capt. Charles Morton, 3rd Cavalry, with family in front of commanding officer's quarters,
1889.
—#1309 Rose Collection, University of Oklahoma Library

Texas Rangers Ben Woodland, Captain Willis, soldier, Harry Robinson, P. S. Carver, Claud Darlington at camp thirty miles downriver from Eagle Pass, Texas.

—R. A. Thompson Collection

Bvt. Lt. Philip Sheridan at Fort Duncan, circa 1855.

—Center for American History, University of Texas at Austin

Brig. Gen. Rufus Shafter, commanded Fort Duncan 1872-1876, 1878-1879.

—National Archives #111-sc-90138

Bridge over Rio Grande at Eagle Pass, circa 1918.

—R. A. Thompson Collection

Standing guard duty under bridge over Rio Grande at Eagle Pass, Texas.
—R. A. Thompson Collection

Bivouac just downriver from bridge at Eagle Pass.
--R. A. Thompson Collection

30th Infantry under canvas at Camp Eagle Pass in 1918.
—Ben Pingenot Collection

Capt. Napoleon B. McLaughlen, 4th Cavalry as brigadier general volunteers, circa 1865.
—National Archives

Brig. Gen. Albert Myer. Father of modern Signal Corps. His first duty station was at Fort Duncan as a physician.
—National Archives

Capt. Charles N. W. Cunningham, 24th Infantry. Served at Fort Duncan.
—National Archives

Officer's quarters, Camp Eagle Pass in 1917.
—Ben Pingenot Collection

24th Infantry (all black) who served at Fort Duncan. Photograph taken elsewhere in 1893.
—From *The Black West* by William Loren Katz

Jesse Sumpter, U.S. Customs Inspector at Eagle Pass, ca. 1894.
—National Archives

1st. Lt. Alfred Collins Markley, 24th Infantry at Fort Duncan.
—National Archives

Capt. James Dorst, 4th Cavalry, served at Fort Duncan as post adjutant.
—U.S. Military History Institute, Carlisle Barracks, Pennsylvania

Group photograph of company of SNIS taken at Fort Clark in 1880s. They all served at Fort Duncan. Front row, 3rd from left, William Shields; 4th from left, Ben July; 5th from left, John July; far right, Sandy Fay; Back row, 3rd from left, Joe Dixson; 4th from left, Ben Wilson.
—Sul Ross University Library

1st Sgt. Ben July with parents Sam and Mary at SNIS camp at Fort Clark.
—Sull Ross University Library

Main street, Eagle Pass, Texas, circa 1885.

—Charles G. Downing Collection

Capt. Charles A. Hartwell, 8th Cavalry, and post commander at Fort Duncan.

—U.S. Military History Institute, Carlisle Barracks, Pennsylvania

Capt. Gustavus Valois, 9th Cavalry, at Fort Duncan.

—U.S. Military History Institute, Carlisle Barracks, Pennsylvania

1st Lt. Peter Boehm, 4th Cavalry, served at Fort Duncan. Awarded Medal of Honor during Civil War.

—National Archives

Bed belonging to John L. Bullis brought to Texas by ship landing at the old port of Indianola, Texas.

—Albert Hausser

Gen. Joseph O. Shelby, CSA, buried his colors in Rio Grande at Fort Duncan while crossing into Mexico rather than surrender his command in 1865.

—Fort Duncan Museum

Bvt. Maj. Gen. Christopher Colon Auger commanded Department of Texas at San Antonio during 1870s.

—Fort Sam Houston Museum

Drugstore in Eagle Pass catering to soldiers in 1917.

—Charles G. Downing Collection

Pompey Factor, SNIS, as old man. Awarded Medal of Honor at Fort Duncan in 1875.
—From *Black Indians: A Hidden Heritage* by W. L. Katz

Cpl. Edwin Lonas, 46th Infantry, at Camp Eagle Pass.
—Francisco Barrientos Collection

Cpl. Benjamin Delahauf Foulois, Company G, U.S. Volunteers in 1898. Pioneered military aviation.
—Fort Sam Houston Museum

"A Practice March In Texas" by Frederic Remington. Painted during a visit to Fort Duncan in 1896.
—Don Swanson Collection

Capt. Lea Febiger, 23rd Infantry, circa 1896 in front of long barracks.
—Ben Pingenot Collection

Fay and Maria July, Seminole Negro Indian Scout, circa 1916, served at Fort Duncan.
                    —Fort Sam Houston Museum

Cpl.. Fay July, left and Pvt. Wm. Shields, SNIS who served at Fort Duncan. —Fort Sam Houston Museum

Sgt. Charles Daniels, SNIS, circa 1907 with daughters. Enlisted at Fort Duncan in 1871.
                    —Fort Sam Houston Museum

Maj. Gen. Robert Alexander was commanding officer of Camp Eagle Pass in 1916.
                    —National Archives
                    #111-sc-53485

U.S. Army Band in 1917.

—Ben Pingenot Collection

1st Lieutenant Foulois, U.S. Army, standing by Wright Type B Scout Biplane at Fort Duncan after longest cross-country flight in history of aviation, March 3, 1911.

—Ben Pingenot Collection

Standing inspection at Camp Eagle Pass in 1915. Oscar Horak is fourth from the right. 17th Infantry.

—Kathy Uland

Brig. Gen. Henry W. Wessells was once stationed at Fort Duncan.

—National Archives #111-B-4899

Graffiti found at Fort Duncan sub-camp within yards of Rio Grande some sixty miles below fort.

—Doug Stalker

Company L, 3rd Infantry, at Camp Eagle Pass, 1915-20. (Photo continues left to right, from top to bottom.)
　　　　　　　　　　　　　　　　　　　　　　　　—Fort Duncan Museum

Fort Duncan parade grounds, circa 1941.

—Fort Duncan Museum

Fort Duncan commanding officer's quarters, circa 1953.

—*San Antonio Express-News*/Ben Pingenot Collection

Kickapoo Indian cane house underneath International Bridge at Eagle Pass in 1984.

—Photo by author

Oscar Horak, center, in cook tent at Camp Eagle Pass in 1915.
                                    —Kathy Uland

Cpl. Raymond Lopez, 46th Infantry, at Camp Eagle Pass in 1920.

—Francisco Barrientos Collection

Sgt. Harvey C. Pollay and bride Sabina Ritchie while stationed at Camp Eagle Pass in 1918.

—C. Gordon Downing

Army recruiters at Camp Eagle Pass in 1918. Notice girls wearing pistols.
                                    —Ben Pingenot Collection

Refugees crossing Rio Grande at Eagle Pass during Mexican Revolution in 1916.
—Francisco Barrientos Collection

Soldiers await arrival of train at Eagle Pass in 1917.
—Charles G. Downing Collection

Gate and marker to Camp Eagle Pass before 1954 flood. Both washed away. Note hospital in background.
—Francisco Barrientos Collection

Gate and marker showing flood waters before washing away.
—Francisco Barrientos Collection

Magazine still standing today and old officer's quarters (now gone) about 1920 at Camp Eagle Pass.

—Francisco Barrientos Collection

Fort Duncan adjutant's office. —Fort Duncan Museum

Fort Duncan commanding officer's quarters.
—Fort Duncan Museum

Boy Scouts meeting at old band hall (EM barracks) in 1930. Mr. Chardy—Sea Scout Master, Mr. B. Ware, Scout Master. Sea Scouts L-R are Raynor Buckley and Richard Juve. Top row Boy Scouts are L-R, Richard Lane, Tom Hall, Wm. Peiper. Middle row L-R are Mr. Ware, Pete Rossi, Jo Bob Kinsel, T. A. Stevenson, Wm. Murray, Key Wesley Ryan, Val Juve, unknown, J. M. Schwartz, Ben Miller, unknown, Mr. Chardy. Bottom row L-R are Jimmie White, John Hawkes, Pete Marinos, Joe Barksdale, Johnnie Johnson, Warren Weisenheimer, Leroy Strogar, ? Anderson, Edward Watkins, John Roy Martin, and Jinx Barksdale. —Pete Rossi

Headquarters Building, Fort Duncan, made of sandstone.
　　—Michael J. Ritchie Collection

Interior of Robert E. Lee Memorial Building at Fort Duncan.
　　—Fort Duncan Museum

Robert E. Lee Memorial Building at Fort Duncan.
　　—Fort Duncan Museum

Lt. Charles G. Downing, officer of the day at Eagle Pass Army Airfield, Christmas 1943.
—Charles G. Downing Collection

Lt. Downing near Lehman Ranch during training, 1943.
—Charles G. Downing Collection

Chapter 4

Peace and a Name Change: 1884-1897

It is an ill wind that blows no one good, and the old post, so often maligned and intended for disuse, was once more resurrected. Disturbances along the Rio Grande near Eagle Pass had increased; horse and cattle stealing had become epidemic with occasional loss of life.[1]

The commanding officer at Fort Clark was directed by Special Order No. 31, Department of Texas, to send one company of infantry to Eagle Pass to establish a post on March 12, 1886. This camp would occupy the old Fort Duncan area.[2]

Less than three years had elapsed since total abandonment of Fort Duncan. Time, though short, had reduced the feeble buildings to ruins, and the more permanent structures required enormous refurbishing. Fort Clark ordered Company K, 19th Infantry to exit its home on Las Moras Creek for a two-day march to Eagle Pass. The company arrived at the wind-blown ruins of old Fort Duncan on April 3, 1886. They had left on April Fool's Day—a fact many would recall in later life.[3]

The new station was to be officially known as Camp at Eagle Pass, not Fort Duncan. From the first day the new camp was a subpost of Fort Clark. On February 10, 1893, the Camp at Eagle Pass became an independent post, but by June 9, 1894, it again came under the umbrella of Fort Clark.[4]

The use of facilities previously recognized as a fort never again reached that grandiose designation.

The development of the military depended on the accumulating national crises. Certainly the Spanish-American War, Philippine Insurrection, Mexican revolution, First World War, and the ensuing border difficulties created a new need for U.S. soldiers near Eagle Pass. It is not surprising that their presence was by national decree until the Camp at Eagle Pass was discontinued in February 1927.

Until that date many activities proved the reemergence of the old fort as justifiable in expense and personnel. The little town across the arroyo grande known as Eagle Pass provided both entertainment and female companionship for many years. I quote Frederic Remington from his short story "When a Document is Official," in which he described young men in barracks: "A young man with increased heart action is going to do something besides standing on one foot leaning against a wall: nature changed that long ago." Sure it is that young men are naturally going to find young women and vice versa. This is part of life and part of the history of Fort Duncan/Camp at Eagle Pass. From the days of Jesse Sumpter in the 1850s to the air force training bases in the early 1940s, the area once known as Fort Duncan became heaven or hell for young men from throughout the United States.

The Camp at Eagle Pass slowly returned some of the ruins to habitable buildings. Capt. Charles Morton, 3rd Cavalry, was placed in command and remained as such, off and on, until 1891.[5]

Interestingly, by 1889 the small post had enlarged to a full company. By August 31, 1889, the official garrison reached fifty-four enlisted of Company A, 3rd Cavalry. However, they were considered on detached service from Fort Clark, and the new camp was really nothing more than a cantonment.

There is really little known or published regarding the first years of reestablishing a post at Eagle Pass. The initial reports subject to Fort Clark scrutiny finally arrived at Department of Texas Headquarters at Fort Sam Houston, Texas (San Antonio). The commanding officer of that department was again D. S. Stanley, albeit by 1889 a brigadier general.[6]

Stanley, an old soldier and graduate of the Military Academy in 1852, had been awarded the Medal of Honor at Franklin,

Tennessee, in 1864 and was severely wounded while serving as a corps commander during the rebellion.[7]

The government was still paying $75 monthly in rental to John Twohig of San Antonio while debating the old reservation's need and accountability.[8]

Stanley prevailed, and the quartermaster general's office directed the army to obtain the title to the old Fort Duncan reservation. Of course, years would elapse before any governmental entity would act. In the meantime, the camp remained a one-company post from 1886 through 1894. The 3rd Cavalry switched companies, now called troops, from Fort Clark with regularity.

On February 10, 1893, Camp at Eagle Pass became once more an independent post answering to the department commander at San Antonio. However, this heady independence was short-lived. Due to reluctance to again submit large expenses for another post on the Rio Grande and professional grumbling regarding duplication of command interests, orders for separation were revoked on June 9, 1894, and Camp at Eagle Pass returned as an official subpost of Fort Clark.[9]

Brief interludes of activity remained in store for the old-new station. Build-up and departure of units destined for the Caribbean and Philippine archipelago began in early 1898 and continued through the turn of the century. The Spanish-American War and Philippine Insurrection saw a great many of those soldiers whose careers had once placed them on the Rio Grande.

Postwar activity dwindled while the republic to the south seethed with revolutionary zeal. By 1913, units were being posted to Eagle Pass with regularity, and cavalry and infantry patrols and marches brought new activity and troops. In 1916 the president mobilized the nation's National Guard, and Camp at Eagle Pass exploded with men and material. At one time over 10,000 troops encamped on and about old Fort Duncan.[10]

Eagle Pass enjoyed enormous prosperity as the post's mission was maintenance of law and order on the border and protection of its citizens from bandits and thugs who sought to use the cloak of revolution for their nefarious activities.

Then the world was shattered by the European conflict. Unable to refrain from participation, President Woodrow Wilson ordered an American Expeditionary Force to France in mid-1917.

Saboteurs and provocateurs mingled in Mexico and attempted various setbacks for allies from that neutral nation. The Camp at Eagle Pass was a prime post for breaking up any sabotage for the vital port of entry at Eagle Pass. Further, all precaution was taken to prevent any seizure of customs or disruption of commerce at the port by German agents. Once more those lonely seven hills served as emplacements for machine guns and troops to forcefully repel any German invaders from the Mexican Republic.[11]

After the war to end all wars, border outposts became superfluous; inevitably, the long life of Fort Duncan/Camp at Eagle Pass was relegated to abandonment. It did exist for another ten years before disuse and uncommon lack of need forced closure by February 1927.[12]

Let us examine some of the attributes of Camp at Eagle Pass, its troops and its mission after Fort Duncan ceased to be in 1883.

One item of extreme importance but little known or appreciated is the significant fact that it was the oldest cooperative weather station in Texas. Records of weather observations began almost at once after the opening of Fort Duncan in 1849. The National Weather Service on November 15, 1991, recognized the city of Eagle Pass for this enormous contribution to the safety and lives of border Texans.[13] A thermometer house had been situated beside the post hospital in 1849 to begin the first weather observation in Texas.

The post had been rented from the Twohig estate for years and by 1892 was paying $900 annually.[14] Because of Brigadier General Stanley's insistence, Congress had allocated $20,000 to purchase the site of old Fort Duncan in 1891.[15] As usual the government action required years to bring fruition to the intention. One factor in the delay was a cloudy deed since suit was in progress on the Twohig estate. However, on July 21, 1894, purchase was finally made, as follows:

> A site for a military post has been purchased at Eagle Pass, Texas (Old Fort Duncan), under the provisions of the act of March 3, 1891. The title papers were submitted to the Attorney General. The following reservation has been transferred to the Interior Department for disposition . . . under the Act . . ., a site . . . containing 155.34 acres has been purchased . . . at a cost of $20,000.00.[16]

Incredible as it seems, since its beginnings nearly a half century earlier, the actual land used for the post was now owned by the government.

In 1892 Capt. H. W. Wessells, Jr. commanded the post and one company of the 3rd Cavalry, sixty men with one lieutenant and one medical officer. Company H, 18th Infantry was also in camp with thirty-eight enlisted and two officers. Much of the year was spent scouting up and down the Rio Grande by the cavalry. In early January, the bulk of the cavalry marched to El Indio and set up housekeeping. Since the road was in good shape toward Laredo and its Fort McIntosh, those patrols generally were in that direction and usually as far as Twin Mountains or Sauz Ranch. Many patrols consisted of four to seven privates with either a corporal or sergeant in command. They would leave Indio with rations for six days and cover 110 to 145 miles on their scouts.[17]

Many bandits-revolutionaries existed in this area during the 1890s, and those following a rogue Mexican named Garza were especially troublesome. The cavalry units participating in the field at that time proved successful, and General Order #6, Department of Texas, is highly complimentary of the 3rd's effort, suppressing the bandits. Garza was active around Piedras Negras in October 1891.[18]

A report of Surgeon General Sutherland in 1892 informed the secretary of war that conditions at "Camp Eagle Pass, Texas . . . are exceedingly unsatisfactory. Windstorms blow the dust through many crevices, the roofs leak and are infested with bats, centipedes and scorpions, while skunks and snakes . . . beneath floors."

Included with the above are the reports of Lt. Ogden Rafferty. One report was not only picturesque but poignant.

> These buildings were originally built about 1849 . . . foundation alone mark the sites of some . . . others have been abandoned as insecure, . . . those in use have been rudely patched in vain effort to make them fit for white people . . . it was necessary to kill a snake 6 feet in length and 8 inches in circumference . . . another snake crawled out from beneath the chairs of the family sitting . . .[19]

Another example of the surgeon general's incredulity is this one: "accommodations are of the most primitive character. Camp at Eagle Pass, Texas had one bathtub for a troop of cavalry . . ."[20]

Bathing, if at all, was normally done in the Rio Grande. The water supply was derived from wells sunk in the riverbanks. The post obtained water by inducing mules or horses to haul water from the river in barrels, which were then apportioned to empties along each company street. Dysentery was endemic. The lieutenant in a final report of angst urgently requested water pipes from the City of Eagle Pass to the camp so as to "furnish a bath and a glass of clear water to all." [21]

By June 1893 the 3rd Cavalry changed stations with Company F, 5th Cavalry then serving at Fort Clark. The cavalry, from several seasoned regiments posted at Clark, would regularly change from that post to Camp at Eagle Pass.

One of the strangest and most humorous incidents, albeit potentially serious, occurred during this first stay of the 5th Cavalry. One of Company F's lieutenants was Lester W. Cornish. He moved his growing family to one of the pitiful officers' quarters, where his wife began housekeeping and caring for their four young children. Since the post barely held more than fifty to sixty souls at this time, the children found amusement anywhere they could escape from their mothers. As most military "brats" will, they pestered the soldiers and marched and mimicked them while responding to bugle calls like their adult alter-egos.

An obsolete cannon sat majestically on the parade ground near the flagpole. One day as Cornish's two sons, Ted and L. Roy, were playing cannon, they found an unusually nice-sized round stone. Let the reader be aware that the cannon served two purposes. One, to fire sufficient powder in a blank to acknowledge each day's lowering of the flag at evening retreat; and two, to warn the post in case of fire. Needless to say, the cannon was thoroughly primed with powder at all times.

The boys, looking for excitement and with immature impatience, decided to load the rock into the cannon. After doing so they playfully forgot that mischief as all manner of new play absorbed their attention.

At the end of the day, the small detail whose job was to sound evening retreat lowered the flag, marched smartly to the flagpole, and took their positions. Soldiers and their families came briskly to attention, and as the flag was furled from its fluttering descent the gunner pulled the lanyard or string which fired the small piece.

Improbable as it seems, the old field piece "reared up on its hind legs" and heaved that rock straight across the Rio Grande amidst several Mexican women and deep into the riverbank mud.

The retreat detail were aghast as they watched helplessly the trajectory of the unknown loaded weapon. Gravity was kind enough to bring the missile to earth without harm, but the women, believing themselves attacked by the might of United States artillery, hastily dug up the rock and raced to the *alcalde* and *policia* with shrieks of fear and exclamation of impending war.

Then occurred a formal demand by the Mexican consul at Eagle Pass to the commanding officer at the camp to explain the sneak attack on the citizenry of a friendly republic. Officialdom in formal correspondence between Washington and Mexico kept the telegraph operator breathless from exertion. Lieutenant Cornish was reprimanded, as was his commander. With final explanation from two terrified little boys and their considerable tears, "both nations agreed to forget the incident with proper diplomatic expertise." [22]

The 5th Cavalry continued the constant patrolling from Eagle Pass toward Laredo. As the 3rd had done, their destination, personnel, and length of marches remained similar.

By October of 1893, a new assistant acting adjutant general for the Department of Texas was stationed at Fort Sam Houston in San Antonio. His name was Maj. Arthur MacArthur, former Civil War hero, Medal of Honor recipient, and the father of Douglas MacArthur, about whom nothing need be added. [23]

One interesting unit posted to Camp at Eagle Pass from Fort Clark was Company G, 7th Cavalry. This outfit arrived May 15, 1894, replacing Company F, 5th Cavalry. Now up to strength, it was still commanded by Capt. W. S. Edgerly, who with that company withstood the onslaught of thousands of Sioux and Cheyenne warriors while holding part of the Reno entrenchment at the Battle of the Little Big Horn, Montana, June 25-26, 1876. Exactly six months later this famous company returned to its regular duties at Fort Clark. [24]

December 1894 brought a name change to the post. Henceforth, at least officially, it was to be called Outpost Camp Eagle Pass, Texas. Of further interest, although the post was constantly garrisoned by cavalry, all scouting patrols were discontinued. This appears odd, but perhaps horseflesh and grain for animals and extra rations to keep men in the field became a superfluous expense in that time of peace. Certainly the border area was quiet and lacking in sufficient excitement to justify field operations.

The new year of 1895 continued to see Troops F and B, 5th Cavalry exchanging stations between Fort Clark and Outpost Camp at Eagle Pass.

On May 23, 1895, an old friend returned after twenty-five years when he was the officer commanding Fort Duncan. General Order #11, Department of Texas, provided for a change of command to that department. The new commander was Brig. Gen. Zenas R. Bliss.[25] Remembering his service on the border, one of the first instructions given was to limit any unit to a maximum of two years while stationed at the post at Eagle Pass. His comments included the harshness of weather, decaying barracks, and lack of amenities in those more modern times.[26]

That same year of 1895 saw a change of command of the United States Army. October 8 was the date designated for ceremonies to take place in Washington, D.C. Lieutenant General Schofield retired and was replaced by Maj. Gen. Nelson A. Miles. Receipt of his third star was nothing more than a quick Senate approval vote. Miles proved to be a decent administrator if not exemplary.[27]

Some controversy was exhibited a few years later concerning the expeditionary commander to Cuba in 1898. A previous Fort Duncan commander, William R. Shafter, wearing two stars, received the assignment. Shafter's obesity and requirement of a wagon and team for transportation elicited several unsavory comments.

By year's end the post was selected to house a company of infantry. The 5th Cavalry, no longer required for active field work, returned to Fort Clark and was replaced by Company D, 23rd Infantry, commanded by Capt. Lee Febiger. Their arrival on December 11, 1895, barely allowed time to acclimate from a cavalry post to one of infantry.[28]

Of considerable interest is the arrival in January of the famous sculptor, artist, and writer, Frederic Remington. He had come to Outpost Camp at Eagle Pass at the invitation of Captain Febiger for a quail hunt. The train arrived from San Antonio, and Remington repaired to his host's quarters, where he was warmly received by the captain and his wife and children.[29]

Excitement of the hunt caused both men to arise early the next morning. One of the children, a boy named Paul and still a crawling baby, had innocently wandered close to Remington's bed and picked up his loaded pistol, stuck it in his mouth, and began to gum the hard barrel for a teething ring. Remington was stunned and unable to move for fear the gun might fire. Fortunately, Mrs. Febiger, accustomed to finding unhealthy objects in the baby's mouth, gently removed the pistol, and all heaved a sigh of relief from what appeared to be imminent tragedy.[30]

While spending a few days at the post, Remington painted several scenes. One called "A Practice March in Texas" appeared in his book *Crooked Trails*. That march consisted of the captain, a lieutenant, and forty-four enlisted men. They prepared for field service and were in "Heavy Marching Order." This included haversacks with three days of rations, rolled blanket around the shoulder (which housed their change of clothing), personal items, and a shelter half or one side of a pup tent, canteen, and rifle. Four privates and one musician, with Cpl. John Reeves in charge, rode bicycles to act as couriers as no other transportation made the march.

That specific march was a round trip to the Nueces River below Uvalde, Texas, and required nine days to travel an official 129 miles, March 21-30, 1896.[31]

June 19, 1896, brought General Order No. 24 from the Department of Texas stating reciprocal crossing of the Rio Grande would allow either U.S. or Mexican troops to chase hostile Indians.[32] That seemed hardly necessary in 1896, but obviously both governments wished to show good intentions and harmony toward each other.

Later in the year, 2nd Lt. J. G. Harbord, 5th Cavalry, arrived with three enlisted men to survey the post. This was accomplished by October 28, 1896. Harbord went on to command a very active 2nd Division during World War I and served as chief of staff.[33]

Another officer who would go on to fame and had previously served at Forts Clark and Duncan was the intrepid quartermaster of the 4th Cavalry under Mackenzie, Henry Ware Lawton. He visited the post at Eagle Pass on February 20, 1897, as inspector general of the Department of Texas.[34] Now a lieutenant colonel, Lawton inspected each of the military garrisons in his department every year for proper usage of material and any glaring deficiencies in command or personnel.

It was Lawton who met the troops returning from Mexico after the Remolino expedition in 1873. His arrival with rations for horses and men was met with open displays of tears and hoarse cries of gratitude.[35] Again, during the Red River Campaign in 1874, it was Lawton who miraculously managed to have his trains moving and serving the large command. He was hand-picked by General Miles to lead the campaign against Geronimo and was highly instrumental in bringing that Apache and his followers out of Mexico to Skeleton Canyon in Arizona for surrender.[36] He served in Cuba in 1898, as a major general of volunteers, and was killed in action in the Philippines campaign. Lawton, Oklahoma, is named for this fine officer who served his country from the Civil War until his death nearly forty years later.[37]

The 23rd Infantry remained the garrison's one-company strength, alternating companies from Fort Clark during 1896, 1897, and early 1898. They did little more than show the flag. Practice marches of twice a year were usually in light marching order and traveled to Devils River and return. Usually, one officer and forty-seven enlisted men, many times Company D, concluded an eighteen-day march of 195 miles.[38] They would return shortly after pay day, which occurred on the 27th or 28th of each month.[39]

War clouds had been signaled to all posts with regular army units by early 1898. The Spanish-American War literally denuded many frontier posts in the escalating crisis. Mobilization was hurried and left much to be desired, but these problems proved a godsend nineteen years later, having been corrected so that world war manpower was more readily expedited.

Outpost Camp at Eagle Pass was reduced to one officer and enlisted men on April Fool's, 1898. The 23rd Infantry in almost its entirety was telegraphed instructions from Headquarters, Department of the Gulf, to entrain for field duty at New Orleans. 1st Lt. Benjamin C. Morse, 23rd Infantry, and two privates remaining from his company manned the post in somewhat of a silly exercise.[40]

Chapter 5
Spain and Then Mexico: 1898-1916

Camp Eagle Pass became home to the 3rd Texas Volunteer Infantry. This unit existed to keep law and order at outlying military stations within the state. 1st Lt. Charles H. Moody assumed his new command May 25, 1898.[1] By June he was reinforced by his full company. Several of those companies garrisoned Fort Clark and Camp at Eagle Pass. Companies B and M, 3rd Texas Volunteers, traded back and forth during the year.

In January 1899 the ambassador from Mexico died in Washington and his remains were ordered to enter Mexico at Eagle Pass. Accordingly, the commanding general, Department of the Gulf, ordered Company M, 3rd Texas Volunteer Infantry, now under federal service, to act as guard of honor. At the depot in Eagle Pass a detachment of this unit under Lt. E. G. Abbot fired a seventeen-gun salute with three-inch field pieces. A guard of honor under the command of Lt. Thomas N. Adams composed of sergeants Regan, Lovejoy, Keesee, Harris and Bonnos, Corporals Cassaty, Stanford, Scott, Moore, Lunsford, Womack, Shaw and Sturgis, accompanied the casket to Piedras Negras.[2]

Company M, 3rd Texas Volunteer Infantry, was dutifully mustered out of the federal service February 16, 1899, their need completed as the war emergency was canceled.[3]

As the war waned in the Caribbean, U.S. troops began returning to the States and as usual the cry for demobilization was loud
and clear. Many fine regular regiments, decimated more by tropical
disease than combat, became destined to lose much of their
strength through forced attrition.

The 10th Cavalry was one of those regiments selected for re-
duction. The first contingent of that heroic regiment of black soldiers and white officers arrived at Camp Eagle Pass February 17,
1899, under the command of 2nd Lt. Henry C. Whitehead.[4]

Although mostly in ruins, the old post with a little clean-up
served as the mustering-out station for a large group of cavalrymen.
The garrison provided twenty men minimal police duty while their
numbers were depleted by discharges. General Order No. 40,
Adjutant General, Department of the Gulf telegraphed discharge
notices February 26, 1899.[5]

On June 1, 1899, those remnants of the once proud 10th
Cavalry were replaced by those from the 9th Cavalry, the only other
all-black cavalry regiment with white officers in the U.S. Army.
They too were reduced by discharge, and a small garrison under the
command of 2nd Lt. George Van H. Moseley maintained the post.
Moseley was required to spend time at Fort Clark, so the only offi-
cer left at Camp Eagle Pass was Acting Assistant Surgeon Malone
Duggan, U.S. Army.[6]

After May 1899 two Seminole Negro Indian Scouts were per-
manently assigned to Camp Eagle Pass. Almost thirty years had
elapsed since first those scouts were recruited to track and destroy
hostile Indians from their base at old Fort Duncan. They were mid-
dle-aged now. One who had served there and at Fort Clark during
the 1870s was Billy July.[7]

Their primary leader and Indian fighter, John Lapham Bullis, a
major and department paymaster in July 1899, returned to his old
post where in 1873 as a second lieutenant, 24th Infantry, Lieutenant
Colonel Shafter had appointed him chief of scouts at Fort Duncan.[8]
Fully twenty-five engagements with hostile Indians are attributed
to Bullis, mostly just he and a few scouts involved. His story is incredible and his exploits trailing and fighting superior numbers
would shame Victor Hugo's famous detective, Inspector Jaubert
from *Les Miserables*. Bullis and his Seminole Negro Indian Scouts

deserve a large book, and hopefully time will reveal a long-awaited recital of these men.

October 1899 saw seventeen enlisted men of the 9th Cavalry with four hospital stewards and the acting assistant surgeon as total manpower for the post. The last month of the year was similar in a token garrison with the same troops, all Troop M, 9th Cavalry. Lieutenant Moseley, two scouts, and the same two enlisted men from Company D, 23rd Infantry who had been left behind the year before when the rest of their company shipped out completed the manpower.[9]

The new century began with the above, and by February 1900, 2nd Lt. Thomas A. Roberts and twelve enlisted of Troop H, 10th Cavalry arrived. This new command came from a special order of the commanding officer at Fort Clark, and the relieved 9th Cavalry troopers returned to Brackettville.[10] This small detachment remained at Camp Eagle Pass with a new commander, Capt. Robert D. Reed, Jr., 10th Cavalry. The post remained a sub-post of Fort Clark under the direct command of the commanding officer of that fort from July 7, 1900, until February 15, 1902. The officers at Camp Eagle Pass commanded only their small detachment, not the post.[11]

For the next four years numerous units were designated by special order of "Commander, Fort Clark" to furnish detachments for Camp Eagle Pass. As they rarely exceeded eighteen total their presence was strictly janitorial and for protection of government property.[12]

Those units involved included the Artillery Corps, U.S. Army, 12th Cavalry (five new cavalry regiments authorized as regulars to counter personnel requirements for that service due to the Spanish-American War and the Philippine Insurrection), and the 4th, 12th, and 26th Infantry regiments. All these detachments moved freely back and forth from Fort Clark and by order of its commander.[13]

In July 1902, Fort Clark received most of the 12th Cavalry. The post commander was Maj. Luther R. Hare, 12th Cavalry. Hare had been Custer's chief of scouts for the Powder River Campaign and survived with Reno and Benteen's command at the Little Big Horn affair. He had finally been promoted out of his old regiment, the 7th Cavalry.[14]

Camp Eagle Pass during 1900-1904 sustained a detachment of

twelve enlisted and one officer. Most of the year 1901 saw detachments from Troops B and C, 12th Cavalry and those were changed every thirty days. Enlisted were always composed of one sergeant, one corporal, and ten privates. A professional scavenger was hired by the quartermaster department at Clark for $20 month to skulk about the old post and Eagle Pass environs, seeking whatever was necessary to keep the gates open.[15]

Early spring arrived at border Texas in February and a detachment of twenty-six enlisted under command of 1st Lt. Halstead Dorey, 26th Infantry, arrived to spell the cavalry. Two scouts were still attached to the post, but apparently had no active duties. Tradition dies hard in the service and it is presumed the War Department was determined to anticipate the need for scouts in the event hostiles became prominent.

Once again, Camp Eagle Pass, nee Fort Duncan, was summarily dismissed from having further military usage. The post of over 150 acres, albeit now owned by the government, was considered expendable. How many times in the nearly half century of existence had other generals sought to diminish accomplishments and ridicule the crude living conditions so often criticized by privates and officers alike?

The Department of Texas ordered abandonment of Camp at Eagle Pass, and the commanding officer at Fort Clark was ordered to issue the directive. 1st Lt. Robert K. Spiller, 26th Infantry had commanded the last detachment from March 2 to April 1, 1904.[16]

Camp Eagle Pass began the inevitable decay, rot, and vandalism. The description of Camp Eagle Pass, Texas in the War Department's annual update for 1904 offered several interesting points. A summary of the post buildings included "4 officers' quarters, 2 NCO quarters, 1 stableman's, 1 hospital (5 beds), 1 barracks (60 men), 1 administration building, 1 chapel, PX, day-room and library (one building), 1 guardhouse, 1 corral (94 animals), 1 commissary, 1 bakery, 1 magazine, 2 shops and 1 grainery."[17]

Mineral oil lamps provided the post lighting. Water was housed in one 10,000-gallon water tank; there was no post sewer. The cemetery had been abandoned in 1900, with all remains being exhumed and moved to the National Cemetery in San Antonio. All burials since then were made at the Fort Clark, Texas, cemetery.[18]

Time and the exigencies of circumstances in Mexico required the U.S. government to discreetly monitor activities along its southern borders. Mexico was aflame with revolution, and names such as Pancho Villa, Emiliano Zapata, Obregon, Madera, Carranza, and Huerta became as commonplace at Eagle Pass as in Mexico. Fighting between different factions and the government of Porfirio Diaz was continuous and moved north and south through the central states of Mexico with total abandon.

The United States, sole owner of an abandoned military post on the Rio Grande at Eagle Pass, Texas, decided to place a small group of military specialists from a detachment of the Signal Corps, Company A, U.S. Army onto the decayed post February 9, 1911.[19]

The seven years preceding abandonment of Camp at Eagle Pass had proven extremely unkind to the property. Neglect, vandalism, and outright theft had left the old post dangerously close to extinction. Several of the old buildings were made serviceable, and for the first time in the post's history, a typewriter was used on the station's monthly records.[20]

Apparently these signalmen were able to obtain classified information through their rather unsophisticated wireless sets that prompted the War Department into action. What was determined is not available to the author. Supposition would dictate fear of border incursions by Mexican revolutionists. Determined to remain neutral, the U.S. government was just as determined to protect its citizens on the border who conceivably would be in harm's way. Therefore, Troop A, 3rd Cavalry was detached from Fort Clark and instructed to take station at Camp Eagle Pass.[21]

With one officer, fifty-four enlisted, and five extra horses, this unit marched to Eagle Pass the first week of March 1911. They were there scarcely two weeks when a desertion in the ranks occurred. Pvt. Arthur Coleman, 3rd Cavalry, deserted his post March 25, 1911. Without further comment the record shows Coleman's file as "Worthless."[22]

The Signal Corps maintained a small detachment through 1914 and was in wireless communication constantly between Eagle Pass and Minera, Texas, near Laredo.

The year 1911 was both historic and prophetic of the future by an amazing incident at Camp Eagle Pass. An adventurous young army officer by the name of Benjamin Foulois (Fa-loy), then a first lieutenant, represented all that later became the U.S. Air Force.

He was completely confident that aviation would become a prominent and necessary arm of the military. By February 1910, Foulois, mostly self-taught, had encouraged and persuaded the army to buy an aircraft, and at Fort Sam Houston, Texas, he began his education in flying from that post's parade ground. The aircraft, such as it was, was officially designated Signal Corps Airplane No. 1.[23]

The situation in Mexico was rapidly enlarging, and Foulois intended using his aircraft for observation. At that time, due to patriotism and excellent public awareness techniques, Robert Collier of *Collier's* magazine loaned his newer and larger Wright aircraft to the army and Foulois. With the aircraft came an experienced test pilot named Phil Parmalee. His duty was to offer instruction to Foulois. These two pilots immediately went aloft. The *San Antonio Express* described that historical significance by declaring the flight as the first ever to have two people aloft in the same aircraft.

Through proper channels, permission was given to fly observation patrols along the Rio Grande, and the aircraft was crated and hauled to Fort McIntosh at Laredo, Texas. Here it was assembled and prepared for the initial cross-country flight to Eagle Pass. Should disaster strike the pilots were informed the wagon road to Eagle Pass was "corroded and marred with deep arroyos." At 2:00 P.M. on March 3, 1911, the aircraft with Foulois and Parmalee on board took off and headed upriver, their only navigational aid. At Minera, only a few miles from Laredo, and where wireless communication was possible to Eagle Pass, the aircraft was spotted and duly noted.[24]

Eighteen miles below Eagle Pass at Indio Ranch, Mr. Allen, the ranch manager, was entertaining his grandchildren, two of whom were Eagle Passans: Lorena Eichelberger and Francis Conlon. The astonishment and excitement generated by the flying machine passing overhead cannot be calculated.[25]

The Scout biplane with an altitude of about 800 feet soon created even more incredulity over the town of Eagle Pass. Spotting the dilapidated buildings and parade ground of Camp Eagle Pass, the pilots landed at 4:07 P.M. that eventful Friday. Immediately, throngs of onlookers arrived and a corporal with both sidearm and rifle was ordered to guard the aircraft.

This flight had broken the world's record for distance, covering nonstop 106 miles in two hours and ten minutes. Not only that, but the aircraft was the very first to land at Eagle Pass. Certain it is that the age of military aviation began with this flight.

It is interesting to note that the return trip was equally exciting. Returning downriver, an accidental improper use of the mechanical apparatus caused the engine to quit, and the airplane splashed ignominiously upside down in the Rio Grande, not too far from the Indio Ranch. Young Mike Wipff rode quickly to the riverbank and found both pilots alive but wet and cold. He was asked by Foulois to bring help from Camp Eagle Pass. Soldiers from a small observation post at Indio finally disassembled the plane and brought it to shore, where an army wagon loaded it and the fliers and returned them to Camp Eagle Pass. The aircraft was repaired and flown again.[26] The two pilots, civilian Parmalee and Lieutenant Foulois, survived other such minor irritants until Parmalee was killed in a crash. Foulois went on to become a major general and chief of the Army Air Corps.[27]

The next three years brought little excitement and but a handful of soldiers as itinerant caretakers to Camp Eagle Pass. But when revolution in Mexico enflamed that country and its population, the army recognized the unique placement of the old camp and decided prudence was necessary with the immediate threat of revolution spilling over into the United States. An ugly, unpleasant incident between U.S. forces and Mexicans at Vera Cruz in 1914 exacerbated the problems between both republics, and the army ordered Lt. Col. Thomas W. Griffith, 17th Infantry, to take his regiment to Camp Eagle Pass.[28] Because of the seriousness of the situation Griffith was reinforced by Battery C, 3rd Field Artillery. Immediately, the camp became home to over 1,000 officers and men. The old post was staggered trying to house men and animals. The buildings, long unused and deteriorated, could not be utilized, and the camp became a tent city. Griffith arrived March 21, 1914, and his regiment remained through April, 1916. By January 1915, the 17th Infantry was joined by Battery F, 6th Field Artillery and twenty-four men of the Quartermaster Corps.[29]

The year 1916 was highly unusual in that the European conflict seemed inevitably to bring the United States into conflict. Moreover, the chaos in Mexico had indeed required enormous intervention by armed American soldiers. After much provocation, President Wilson signaled his approval, and Brig. Gen. John Pershing was ordered to take the field in pursuit of Mexican irregulars who had invaded Columbus, New Mexico, on March 9, 1916.[30]

Almost 10,000 American regular army troops crossed the international boundary in a punitive expedition. Such was the seriousness of the crisis and without doubt a realization of mass troop concentration needed shortly in Europe, that the president called to active duty all National Guard troops for service near the Mexican border.[31]

Literally tens of thousands of guardsmen began entraining from states all over the Union, and many thousand came to Camp Eagle Pass.

The 17th Infantry departed and was replaced by the 19th Infantry on May 1, 1916. Only Companies A and B arrived, bringing six officers and 114 enlisted. The battery of field artillery and the quartermaster troops still remained as garrison.[32]

The famous 3rd Infantry arrived June 1, 1916, enlarging the post by nearly a thousand. What is interesting is that most of the officers and men of the Coast Artillery Corps, commonly called C.A.C., arrived and took station.[33] One squadron of the 14th Cavalry and its headquarters personnel further swelled the camp with more men, horses, and mules.[34]

Among those officers of the 3rd Infantry who would rise to such prominence a quarter century later in World War II were 2nd Lt. James A. Van Fleet and 1st Lt. Walter Kruger, both of whom became general officers. Van Fleet went on to lead forces in the Korean action.[35]

The post, now bursting with men and material, was swollen again in August 1916 by twenty-six officers and 616 enlisted of the 30th Infantry. Company A, 19th Infantry was pushed to the Elm Creek Bridge and lived literally in the field.[36]

The following were stationed at Camp Eagle Pass on field duty in mid-May of 1916: 3rd Infantry Regiment including Headquarters and Machine Gun Company; Headquarters and 2nd Squadron, 14th Cavalry; Radio Detachment Company E, Field Signal Corps.[37]

All orders originated from the War Department for these

movements but came direct by telegraph from Headquarters, Southern Department, Fort Sam Houston, Texas (San Antonio).

Company A, 3rd Infantry was sent to Indio Ranch and Company M, 3rd Infantry went north to Lehmans Ranch, the former downriver from Eagle Pass.[38] A detachment of sixteen men of Company I, 3rd Infantry relieved Company E, 19th Infantry at the Elm Creek Bridge as they were ordered to take station at Del Rio, Texas.[39]

The Coast Artillery Corps had been ordered by Headquarters, Eastern Department, to Camp Eagle Pass. The 1st Provisional Battalion, C.A.C., arrived in mid-June 1916 and comprised the following: 102nd Company, 130th Company, 134th Company, and 146th Company.[40]

It is not known how this particular unit was chosen for Eagle Pass, but certainly their expertise in stationary fortifications was instrumental in constructing machine-gun emplacements on the surrounding hills. Those trenches were readily seen as late as 1985.

The revolution in Mexico, although destined to take lives and property in that hapless country for five more years, was slowly ceasing to require military intrusion by summer's end, 1916. The National Guard units were released from federal service and returned to their respective state capitals.

Camp Eagle Pass remained well garrisoned by regular army units in case of any spillover by Mexican irregulars and waited for the world's next momentous calamity.

Chapter 6

Guard Duty: 1917-1927

In early February of 1917 the Punitive Expedition emerged from within the Republic of Mexico and crossed the line into the U.S. at Columbus, New Mexico. It was from here that the expeditionary troops began their futile chase of Pancho Villa in March 1916. Although Villa proved elusive to capture, the bandits and irregulars under his command had been thoroughly punished. The Carranza government and its troops could not alter the course of history, and with all-out war imminent in Europe the governments of the U.S. and Mexico realized further animosity by Mexico would result in U.S. occupation of that country.

The National Guard, federalized by President Wilson on June 18, 1916,[1] stood ready all along the border by the tens of thousands with many serving at Camp Eagle Pass.

The last guard mount at Camp Eagle Pass by federalized National Guard troops at the flagpole on the parade grounds was October 1916 by the Kansas National Guard.[2] This state unit boasted the 1st Infantry. Regimental Sgt. Maj. Sam McKone saluted alongside 1st Battalion Adjutant, 1st Lt. Lester Stryker.[3]

Another large contingent of guardsmen stationed at Camp Eagle Pass were from Tennessee. The 1st Tennessee Infantry under Col. Harry S. Berry and Ambulance Company #1 under Capt.

Jerome Morgan remained until early 1917 before entraining for Memphis, where they were mustered-out March 24. These units were known as "Chickasaw Guards."[4]

The 1st and 2nd Regiments of the Kansas National Guard left Fort Riley for Eagle Pass, Texas, on July 6 and arrived at that station July 8 and 9, 1916. Those regiments were transformed into a brigade by adding the 1st Vermont Infantry. Col. Perry M. Hoisington, as senior officer, 2nd Kansas Infantry, commanded.[5] Two squads of the Kansas 1st Regiment went immediately on outpost duty by guarding an abandoned coal mine two miles upriver from Eagle Pass.

For the first time since the Spanish-American War, the Maryland National Guard spent its active duty by being posted to Camp Eagle Pass. They reached Eagle Pass by train in July 1916 and were billeted in tents next to the 30th Infantry (U.S. Regulars).[6]

One of the officers remarked that the time spent on the border was the most uncomfortable in his military life. Training marches were made frequently to Indio Ranch and Spofford, Texas. One full company was assigned to bridge guard duty nightly at both the pedestrian and railroad bridges in Eagle Pass.[7]

Recognizing that the European struggle must inevitably draw America into war, our government utilized the mass concentration of guardsmen for necessary training. Interestingly those troops from Kansas stationed at Camp Eagle Pass made up a full division for a hike from San Antonio to Austin. Over 14,000 men and nearly 700 officers made the march along with 5,140 animals and motorized transports. That division passed in review at Austin before Maj. Gen. Frederick Funston, commanding the Southern Department, which coordinated all operations in Mexico and on the border.[8] As Napoleon wisely said, "War is a business and must be learned like any other profession."

Training at Camp Eagle Pass continued after U.S. entrance into the world war. Even with the stone barracks many personnel inhabited the huge tent city surrounding the original Fort Duncan grounds.

At that time the buildings then in existence at Camp Eagle Pass included rock stables in the shape of a letter U, two wings running north and south and connected by a thick wall at the northern end. A large two-story commissary was crowned with a square cupola on the roof.[9]

To the right of the commissary were the noncommissioned officers' headquarters and beyond it the camp bakery and blacksmith shop. Older Eagle Passans recall the clamor of the anvil and rubbernecking on those days animals were shod.

The huge hay and wood yard lay just beyond the above and provisions were covered by tarpaulins. The hay was soldier-cut from the open range or bought from Dan Wueste, who brought it in from Mexico by oxcart.[10] The hills to the southwest were artillery ranges, and along the Laredo road was the old cemetery.

To the south and southeast of the parade ground was officers' row, all then being built of stone. Some distance farther southwest were a few *jacales* housing the Seminole Negro Indian Scouts. All of the above were standing in 1934, albeit in dilapidated but recognizable condition.[11]

From the beginnings of Fort Duncan when U.S. troops first examined old Pasquatche and the ford used by both Mexicans and Americans, no more bizarre incident occurred than the "Goat War at San Jose." Christmas 1917 had just passed and the thousands of troops were waiting for their overnight passes on New Year's Eve. Training schedules were of little use as both trooper and instructor lacked even perfunctory interest in things military.

For some time thieves and rustlers had been crossing the river near the Indio Ranch, eighteen miles below Eagle Pass. Cattle and goats in small numbers were being missed with considerable regularity. Ranch personnel had carefully followed the tracks of their stolen livestock to an easy ford on the Rio Grande. That their animals were being rustled and taken into Mexico was at once undeniable.[12]

The office of Company M, Texas Rangers at Eagle Pass was none too surprised when at 6:30 P.M., December 29 a phone call from A. H. Allen, manager of the sprawling Indio Ranch, interrupted their supper's digestion. Mr. Allen was adamant. This time the thieves had taken 160 head of goats and driven them into Mexico. He wanted his livestock returned—and diplomatic niceties be damned.[13]

Capt. K. F. Cunningham, commanding the Ranger force, recognized the enormity of risking his Rangers, a state constabulary, to

Mexican government response. He immediately determined the U.S. should legitimize the crossing of an international boundary requested the help of U.S. Cavalry stationed at Camp Eagle Pass. Col. Frederick R. Day, 3rd Infantry, who was the commanding officer, accepted the challenge and ordered three troops of 14th Cavalry and a machine-gun section to Boots and Saddles.[14] Troopers hastily drew ammunition and rations for themselves and twenty pounds of grain for their horses. Although the weather was cool, luckily it was not unpleasant for either man or horse. By now the adjutant had his duty clerk prepare orders for the pursuit and capture of the perpetrators as well as the return of stolen property. Within seven hours Captain Cunningham with twelve Rangers and citizens were resting easy at the Indio Ranch along with the aforementioned cavalry.[15] Allen, muttering obscenities, led the force to the river crossing.

At daylight a combined force of the 2nd Squadron, 14th Cavalry, and Rangers, 150 in all, splashed noisily through the shallows to a low bank in the Republic of Mexico.

Only a mile at the trot, the cavalry in column of fours found the thieves near the outskirts of a small pueblo called San Jose.[16] The trail had been an easy one to follow. Suddenly, without warning, shots were fired from the village. "Prepare to dismount and fight on foot," came a stern order from the cavalry. Quickly and professionally the troops dismounted, every fourth man taking the reins of the three horses from the men in his group and removed them rearward out of fire. Skirmishers were formed by platoons in V formation and methodically returned aimed rifle fire toward their attackers.[17] The Mexicans, unused to such startling interruption of their criminal acts, began to retreat to the adobe structures in the village proper. Firing became general with the Mexicans now hidden in their huts, which included women. The command was given to bring up the machine gun and quickly it was oft-loaded from its animal carrier and brought into action.[18]

The rapid firing of .30-caliber slugs tearing into adobe is a marvelous attention getter. Those who were on the receiving end decided discretion was the better part of valor and hastily left house and village by fleeing through the sand and brush.

Maj. Edward Clifford Wells, who began his cavalry career with the 10th in 1901, reported that although his force suffered no casualties, there were seventeen burials in Piedras Negras and three at

San Jose on New Year's Eve.[19] Three hours after an invasion of Mexico by armed U.S. troops the short-lived punitive expedition recrossed the Rio Grande with all hands and remaining goats.

Of course, the diplomatic exchanges were angry and emotional. Citing any number of outrages committed by U.S. troops, the Mexicans were highly uncomplimentary of U.S. foreign policy.

However, the Carranza government could not force the issue since its borders had proven sanctuary to the miscreants and Washington had kept General Pershing a year in Mexico chasing and fighting Mexican guerrillas and soldiers.

Major Wells' prompt and efficient action was sustained by his superiors, and he was quick to reply to a Mexican official's accusation detailing the killing of one of the village women. Expressing regret if indeed true, Wells "excused the deed by saying that those who keep bad company often suffer." [20]

The 3rd Infantry at Camp Eagle Pass was entertained by the townspeople with weekly socials and dances. The enlisted used the old band rehearsal hall (earlier barracks and recently burned Fort Duncan Club), and nearly all the local girls attended. One young lady eventually caught the eye of Sgt. Harvey C. Pollay, 3rd Infantry, and their marriage in 1917 united that soldier and Sabina Ritchie of Eagle Pass. He elected to be discharged at Eagle Pass on completion of his enlistment and later held a considerable ranching interest in Mexico. Interestingly, their daughter, Jean, married another soldier, Charles G. Downing, after their meeting during the early days of World War II while he was stationed in Eagle Pass.[21]

Training troops for the First World War was the major activity of Camp Eagle Pass in 1918. Yet, there was still the ominous threat of bandit incursions from revolution-torn Mexico. Theft was numerous and fear of bodily harm kept the camp fully garrisoned. It was shortly after war's end that the military, following Foulois' example, decided aviation would be integrated into the army.

As such, military aviation began at Camp Eagle Pass by the addition of Flight A, 90th Aero Squadron. This unit became part of the Army Surveillance Group on July 1, 1919.[22] Originally organized at Kelly Field, Texas (San Antonio), the flight began operations on the border September 2, 1919, and remained at Eagle Pass until June 11, 1920. Aircraft used were the DeHavolind DH-4Bs. After leaving Eagle Pass the flight moved to Del Rio for a year and then to Sanderson, Texas, until the squadron returned to Kelly Field, July 2, 1921.[23]

The Army Surveillance Group's primary mission was to patrol the U.S.-Mexican border, enforcing the neutrality law and deterring further clandestine crossings by bandits and/or revolutionists.[24]

A future Medal of Honor recipient and hero of the Second World War, Lt. Gen. Jimmy Doolittle, was one of the early fliers stationed at Camp Eagle Pass. He was attached to the 3rd Infantry, but when the flight moved to Del Rio he was attached to the 12th Cavalry posted at that city.[25]

No air unit was stationed at Eagle Pass prior to 1919, although border flights from other squadrons were operational near Brownsville in 1915.[26]

The Roaring Twenties would see the final dissolution and abandonment of Camp Eagle Pass. Portions of the 44th Infantry arrived to serve alongside the 3rd Infantry. Lt. Col. Paul Giddings, 3rd Infantry and Col. James H. Bradford, 44th Infantry, alternated at commanding Camp Eagle Pass from 1920 until 1921.[27] The last commander before the old post again was ruled by the commander at Fort Clark was Capt. D.B. Culliname, U.S. Cavalry.[28] His command was terminated March 4, 1922, and a caretaker force was sent to Eagle Pass relieving all regular troops who had been stationed at that post. A small detachment of Medical Corps and Quartermaster Corps remained to keep the hospital and equipment protected, but the usefulness of Fort Duncan-Camp Eagle Pass was forever gone. No more would the citizens of Eagle Pass arise to bugle calls and the tramp of thousands of shod hooves and booted heels.

Some of the Fort Clark enlisted men who served as caretakers at Camp Eagle Pass were Sergeants Artemus H. Hemphill, Satterwhite, and Sam Hoover.[29] A few civilians were allowed to live in the deserted officers' quarters for a rental of $10 monthly.[30]

The military post that stood the test of time and travail slowly disintegrated. Once the rock of the Rio Grande Line of Defense against Indians and bandits, rustlers and filibusters, Camp Eagle Pass nee Fort Duncan ceased to exist in February 1927.[31] Neither the War Department nor Fort Clark, its commanding entity, favored further need. Reasonable use became an anachronism. No attempt was made to forestall inevitable total ruin.

Texas is the poorer for neglecting this antiquity and the heritage generated by countless soldiers who did their duty, who stood to arms when necessary and showed the flag against all pretenders of importance.

Since the Volstead Act, made law in 1920, prohibited alcohol sales, Mexico became a panacea for those who wished to drink legally. While some soldiers and their dependents still remained at Camp Eagle Pass, law and order devolved upon the county sheriff. Only the strong survived.

One of those who did was Albert Hausser. A soldier and law-man, Hausser possessed the entrepreneurial spirit as well. The old post needed fresh eggs, and Hausser cornered the market.

A local newspaper informed the public that 8,000 infertile eggs were sold to the post during the month of July 1928, this being the slow time of the year: "He expects sales to reach eighteen thousand a month by September."[32] This would seem to be an enormous amount of cholesterol for a caretaker garrison, but civilians were moving onto the post very rapidly.

Thus died a military presence existing from the end of the Mexican War in 1849 through the Indian Wars, Spanish-American War, Mexico's revolution, and World War I.

Chapter 7

The End of a Post: 1928-1938

Even caretakers found little to care for in this unusual amalgam of dilapidated and obsolete material. Buildings in disrepair and other facilities such as plumbing deteriorated rapidly. The wooden tent floors that had covered three sides of Eagle Pass in 1916 had long since been broken up and used for building material and firewood by Eagle Passans.

The U.S. Quartermaster Corps ordered its caretakers to close and shutter the buildings and remove all usable material to Fort Clark. This included roofing shingles that somehow had survived the ravages of time and scavengers.[1] Civilians were leaving the post, and with no income or usefulness Camp Eagle Pass ceased to exist under any military supervision by 1919.[2]

Eagle Pass, now claiming itself a city, realized a need for a recreational area and decided to petition the owner of old Fort Duncan (the U.S. government) for its use.

The City Council of Eagle Pass resolved on August 4, 1933, "that such city . . . will care for such land as a public park at the exclusive expense of said city, until the Secretary of War or the President of the United States . . . determine . . . needed for military purposes . . ." Mayor T. R. Jones presided at this special meeting.[3]

As a park the now overgrown parade ground and wind-blown

buildings became an exciting, if not dangerous, playground for city youth. Band concerts were infrequent, but picnics and other care-free events became a much needed respite during the depression. City fathers argued the existence of said park was necessary for the town's inhabitants and its image as a modern and attractive gateway to Mexico.

Five years would pass before either city or War Department would follow up on the inevitable solution. Finally, by order of the Secretary of War, the Quartermaster General of the Army offered for sale at public auction on April 6, 1938, at 11:00 A.M. on the premises, all government-owned land comprising the military reservation known as Camp Eagle Pass, Texas.[4]

The amount of land to be sold equaled 155.29 acres. A deposit of $400 was mandatory before any bid was accepted. The property had been appraised at $3,725 and no sale could be for less than that value.[5]

This property having been part of the original Fort Duncan, founded ninety-four years previously and purchased in 1892 for $20,001, now became the sole property of the City of Eagle Pass by virtue of purchase at auction. The price paid was $3,760.[6] This sum represented the annual upkeep of the post by a caretaker force until total abandonment in 1929.

After the usual waiting period and bureaucratic paper shuffling the deed was duly recorded July 6, 1938, in the minutes of the Eagle Pass City Commission.[7]

The large stone barrack commonly referred to as the "recreation building" became home to a troop of Boy Scouts.[8] This building was adjacent to the present golf course club house. As few other facilities then existed or were capable of housing even minimal activity, it soon became necessary to refurbish the old barrack. Because cost was a prohibitive factor a special meeting of the Eagle Pass City Council was held October 5, 1940, and presided over by Mayor H. F. Harper. It was resolved that the recreation building would be leased in one-year increments to a group of citizens, and it would be called the Fort Duncan Club. The citizens were then designated "caretakers" and as such were financially responsible for the building. Any excess revenue after expenses of the club was to be paid into the city treasury.[9] Until this building was destroyed by fire in 1991, it served many members and guests handsomely.

Yet again war clouds darkened, and the old post would furnish succor to uniformed troops. Shortly after December 7, 1941, and the attack on Pearl Harbor, two companies of cavalry marched to the abandoned post and took up quarters near the recently renovated officers' quarters close by the "recreation building." [10]

Obviously the protection of the important port at Eagle Pass necessitated armed personnel to prevent sabotage or disruption of important services.

Because of the excellent weather around Eagle Pass, the War Department determined to inaugurate a training field for advanced single-engine pilots and selected an area just north of town where the present airfield and industrial park now exist." [11] By November 1942, operations were rapidly reaching fruition. A letter from Col. John H. Bundy, adjutant general at the new base, to George Hollis at the Chamber of Commerce requested the use of the stone barracks (recreation building-Fort Duncan Club). He wanted to house a detachment of military police in order to maintain a twenty-four-hour watch at the border crossing and around Eagle Pass. [12]

Eagle Pass Army Air Fields, although north of town, still maintained a presence throughout World War II. The first class of aviation cadets was officially Class 43-A. [13] Their trainer was the silver-skinned AT-6. Less than two months elapsed, with day and night flying, before the new aviators graduated on January 14, 1943. [14] The second class to graduate, a month later, staged an aerial show climaxed by machine-gun strafing of a cardboard train, delighting crowd, dignitaries, and newsreel camera. [15]

The new unit became known as the 827th Single Engine Flying Training Squadron and graduated hundreds of fighter pilots during the war years. [16]

The Fort Duncan Club became the officers' club, which maintained and improved the old stone barracks. A concrete slab was poured behind the old building, and many festive dances and parties utilized the surroundings while the original club members were encouraged to attend. [17]

Mayor H. T. Harper extended a warm invitation to the army for their use of the old military reservation. With consent of the citizens and advice of his city commission, the mayor offered "Fort Duncan Park" to the War Department for use "as recreation or any other use deemed necessary for troop needs." [18] On January 9, 1942, the former reservation of the U.S. government included "nearly two hundred acres . . . having eight remodeled buildings . . . 15,000 square feet . . . electric lights, water, gas and sewer service . . . baseball diamond . . . and a swimming pool approximately 40' x 80'." [19]

The Maverick County Historical Society, Mrs. C. C. Ostrum, Mrs. S. P. Simpson, and Mrs. A. H. Evans particularly had long wished to establish a museum to honor Robert E. Lee. An old stone building once housing the commissary and ordnance sergeant was designated and a suitable restoration was completed. This structure is known as the Lee Building. [20]

This society eventually spawned the Fort Duncan Restoration Association, which is currently active. Between the two organizations, time, energy, and money have been liberally invested to preserve the buildings now left.

A severe flood carried away the overhead sign for Camp Eagle Pass, but the bridge over that immense arroyo leading from camp to the town of Eagle Pass still survives from 1919 with the inscription "C.Q.M. 1919-1920."

Often condemned and threatened with extinction, the military post founded in 1849 on the east bank of the Rio Grande prevailed with honor and fortitude. No matter the emergency, its garrison met challenges as best it could. Officers of the greatest ability and rank served there in company and field grade positions. Eagle Pass was and is because of this rock of the Rio Grande line of defense. At no other Texas frontier outpost has the American flag shown brighter.

Appendix A

BEXAR COUNTY CENSUS
October 18, 1850
Opposite the Escondido on the Rio Grande River

Name	Age	Sex	Birthplace
Pedro Aquila	33	m	Mex
Barbara Aquila	33	f	Mex
Gudino Calveron, stonemason	46	m	Mex
Francisco Vares	18	m	Mex
Victor Espelo	35	m	Mex
Guadelupa Espelo	26	f	Mex
Juan Alcorta	28	m	Mex
Emila Alcorta	30	f	Mex
Pedro Valdez	25	m	Mex
Juliano Zbaso	30	m	Mex
Victoriano Garman	37	m	Mex
Carlos Valdez	33	m	Mex
Santiago Garcia	50	m	Mex
Andres Malies	27	m	Tex
Jesus Garcia	18	m	Mex
Allen McKensie, carpenter	34	m	Mex
Estavano Gonzales	56	m	Mex
Carmalato Gonzales	14	f	Mex
Felip Alefile, herdsman	28	m	Mex
Santo Reina	30	m	Mex
Miguel Gonzales, carpenter	30	m	Mex
Japita Gonzales	25	f	Mex
Jose A. Gonzales	9	m	Mex
Brino Gonzales	7	m	Mex
Susaro Ramires, stonemason	28	m	Mex
Merceda Ramires	25	f	Mex

Thompson Morris, LCL, Cmdng.	48	m	Pa
Martha B. Morris	35	f	NB
James H. Morris	7	m	NY
Charles A. Morris	5	m	NY
George E. Cooper, asst. surg.	26	m	Pa
Joseph B. Plummer, 1st Lt, Co. K	31	m	Mass
Frances Plummer	26	f	NY
Satterlee Plummer	6	m	Wis
Lydia Plummer	4	f	Mo
Frederick L. Denman, 1st Lt, Co. A	27	m	NY
Samuel H. Reynolds, 2d Lt, Co. A	22	m	Va
James McIntosh, 2d Lt, Co. F	22	m	Fla
Thomas Rioden, Sgt. Maj.	34	m	Canada
John Mills, musician	58	m	Ire
William Brown, musician	26	m	Mo
John B. Hennings, musician	36	m	Ger
James Todd, qm. sgt.	34	m	Pa
Augusto Borsa	21	m	Italy
Louis Castean	35	m	Ger
Guisseppe Chiari	28	m	Italy
James Dunberry	21	m	NY
Domingo Decorbeland	23	m	Spain
Jules Hranz	21	m	Ger
Leopold Lichfeld	21	m	Italy
Jovermier Metere	23	m	Italy
Carl Melti	23	m	Italy
Giome Medi	24	m	Italy
George Spinning	25	m	Ger
John Williams	25	m	Ger
Carl Gress	33	m	Ger
Robert Dyas, drummer	14	m	Ire
Francis Lrr(?), drummer	12	m	NY
Thomas Measles, drummer	13	m	NY
Joseph McKay, drummer	14	m	NY
George Robinson, drummer	15	m	NY
Justin Tonsel, drummer	16	m	NY
Henry Vandycke, fifer	14	m	France
James Bearidall, fifer	14	m	Canada
John Craney, fifer	14	m	Eng
Thomas Dennen, fifer	16	m	Ire
William Lutze, fifer	15	m	NZ
Patrick Manly, fifer	16	m	Ire

Louis Tonsel, fifer	14	m	France
Thomas Drury, sgt.	31	m	Ire
James B. Owings, sgt.	34	m	Va
Arther E. Murphy, qm sgt.	31	m	Ohio
Henry Barkydt, qm stg.	33	m	NZ
Patrick Riley, Cpl.	31	m	Ire
James Shimey, Cpl.	27	m	Ire
James Jones, Cpl.	32	m	Ire
Robert Porter	25	m	NY
Joseph Andrews, pvt.	27	m	Ire
John Barry, pvt.	27	m	Ire
James Crosby, pvt.	25	m	Ire
Ezekiel Conway, pvt.	46	m	Pa
John T. Conway, pvt.	27	m	NZ
James Cavender, pvt.	29	m	Ire
Herman H. Delbriggs, pvt.	23	m	Prussia
Donald Gorden, pvt.	29	m	Scot John
Hunter, pvt.	21	m	Ire
James E. Hicks, pvt.	27	m	Tenn
John Murray, pvt.	32	m	Ire
Michael Mullens, pvt.	32	m	Ire
John Murphy, pvt.	31	m	Ire
Edward Mahon, pvt.	29	m	Ire
Martin Miller, pvt.	33	m	NZ
William McConnell, pvt.	22	m	Ire
James ONeile, pvt.	23	m	Ire
John Readrick, pvt.	27	m	Pa
James Power, pvt.	25	m	Ire
Thomas Rome, pvt.	27	m	Ire
Jesse Robinson, pvt.	28	m	Ohio
Mathew Strobe, pvt.	32	m	Ger
George H. Southerland, pvt.	23	m	NZ
Silas H. Swartz, pvt.	29	m	Va
James Smith, pvt.	29	m	Ire
Thomas Tomkinson, pvt.	28	m	Eng
Hartter Wilson, pvt.	31	m	Ohio
Chester Wood, pvt.	22	m	NZ
Frederick Lunden, pvt.	23	m	Den
William Deardore, pvt.	22	m	Ire
Samuel Price, pvt.	30	m	Pa
Mortimor Cook, pvt. Co. F	24	m	Ohio
James Brown, sgt. Co. F	23	m	NY

James Edwards, sgt. Co. F	24	m	Pa
Joseph Fitzimmons, sgt. Co. F	24	m	Ire
Daniel M. Browner, cpl. Co. F	22	m	NZ
James Harrington, pvt. Co. F	27	m	Ire
Andrew Bayer, musician, Co. F	19	m	Ger
Charles Bucholtz, pvt. Co. F	27	m	Prussia
Davis Cady, pvt. Co. F	23	m	Ind
John Carey, pvt. Co. F	26	m	Ire
John Cavanaugh, pvt. Co. F	33	m	Ire
George Casherwood, pvt. Co. F	26	m	Ire
Samuel B. Cote, pvt. Co. F	23	m	Mass
Thomas Crossley, pvt. Co. F	28	m	Eng
James Dillion, pvt. Co. F	24	m	Ire
Edward Develin, pvt. Co. F	23	m	Ire
William Donavan, pvt. Co. F	20	m	Ire
Thomas Downe, pvt. Co. F	25	m	Ire
Sebastian Easinger, pvt. Co. F	28	m	Ger
Daniel B. Easton, pvt. Co. F	35	m	NZ
James Frame, pvt. Co. F	23	m	Ire
Patrick French, pvt. Co. F	28	m	Ire
Patrick Giffort, pvt. Co. F	20	m	Ire
John Greenar, pvt. Co. F	22	m	Ire
John Hayes, pvt. Co. F	27	m	Ire
Jacob Meeklar, cpl. Co. F	25	m	Ger
Michal Hegan, pvt. Co. F	22	m	Ire
Alexander Hofman, pvt. Co. F	22	m	Austria
John Horgan, pvt. Co. F	27	m	Ire
Adam D. Johnston, pvt. Co. F	32	m	Ire
Simon Leazer, pvt. Co. F	22	m	Ger
Valentine Leonard, pvt. Co. F	28	m	Ger
William Nichols, pvt. Co. F	23	m	NY
Michael McCowne, pvt. Co. F	22	m	Ire
Martin Mulcahy, pvt. Co. F	30	m	Ire
William Rand, pvt. Co. F	21	m	Canada
Timothy Riley, pvt. Co. F	26	m	Ire
George Rigan, pvt. Co. F	23	m	Ire
Frederick Schindler, pvt. Co. F	23	m	Switz
Benjamin F. Vanhorn, pvt. Co. F	32	m	Va
Mathew Walter, pvt. Co. F	26	m	Ire
Patrick Doran, pvt. Co. F	30	m	Ire
John Hein, pvt. Co. F	27	m	Ger
Isaac Keller, pvt. Co. F	34	m	NZ

William Speaks, pvt. Co. F	28	m	Mo
Charles Stevens, pvt. Co. F	34	m	Miss
William Sullivan, pvt. Co. F	23	m	Ire
John K. Hall, sgt.	30	m	Ohio
Edward Ross, sgt.	32	m	NZ
Dominick Levely, sgt.	29	m	Ire
Perry Richardson, sgt.	29	m	NZ
Ross Kennedy, cpl.	32	m	Ire
Jesse M. King, cpl.	26	m	Ind
David Kent, cpl.	23	m	Ire
James Kent, musician	30	m	NZ
Walter Toomey, musician	26	m	Ire
William O. Akurn, pvt.	27	m	Ire
George Ball, pvt.	21	m	Ky
George Burk, pvt.	21	m	Scot
Frederick Burk, pvt.	26	m	Scot
Thomas Banning, pvt.	22	m	Ire
John Cassidy, pvt.	21	m	Ire
Phillip Cook, pvt.	33	m	NC
James Eevey, pvt.	22	m	Ire
Anthony Fisher, pvt.	25	m	Prussia
John Prock, pvt.	26	m	Pa
William Gibson, pvt.	23	m	Md
John O'Grady, pvt.	22	m	Ire
Edward Hagan, pvt.	23	m	Ire
James Higland, pvt.	22	m	Ire
Peter Hewes, pvt.	23	m	Ire
Thomas Madden, pvt.	30	m	Ire
William Martin, pvt.	23	m	Canada
Thomas Nugent, pvt.	26	m	Ire
Patrick Murphy, pvt.	23	m	Ire
Edward McGee, pvt.	22	m	Ire
Edward M. Pike, pvt.	28	m	Ire
James Nugent, pvt.	26	m	Ire
Dennis O'Herrin, pvt.	24	m	Ire
John Pearson, pvt.	26	m	Ire
Lincoln Prate, pvt.	33	m	Mass
George Reynolds, pvt.	25	m	Eng
Arthur Sharpley, pvt.	25	m	Ire
Conrad Sill, pvt.	34	m	Ger
John L. Smith, pvt.	39	m	Pa
William W. Smith, pvt.	21	m	Pa

George West, pvt.	23	m	Ire
John Buffington, pvt.	28	m	Va
Berry Duff, pvt.	20	m	Tenn
William Nichols, pvt.	22	m	NZ
Ann Ross, laundress	24	f	Ire
Catherin Murray, laundress	30	f	Ire
John Murray	4	m	NJ
Arthur Murray	2	m	Tex
Margaret Toomey, laundress	35	f	Ire
Catherin Miller, laundress	23	f	Ire
George Miller	9	m	NJ
Henry Miller	4	m	Mo
Ellen Fitzimmons, laundress	20	f	Ire
Sophia Keller, laundress	26	f	Switz
Maria Gress, laundress	38	f	Ger
Charles Gress	4	m	Tex
Catherin Bayer, laundress	22	f	Mex

Appendix B

Soldiers Reinterred National Cemetery
San Antonio, Texas
May 7, 1900

The following were originally buried at Fort Duncan or Camp
Eagle Pass:

Name	Rank	Unit	Date of Death
Noah Hardeson	Pvt.	41st Inf.	9/13/1869
Thomas Baker	Pvt.	24th Inf.	2/24/1870
Milford Harrison	Pvt.	24th Inf.	3/05/1870
Geo. Bradford	Pvt.	24th Inf.	9/17/1870
John Price	Pvt.	41st Inf.	9/27/1870
William Jones	Pvt.	25th Inf.	4/10/1872
Lerois Torbet	Pvt.	24th Inf.	6/18/1872
Robert Emory	Pvt.	9th Cav.	7/04/1872
Enos Murray	Pvt.	25th Inf.	7/07/1872
Israel Williams	Pvt.	9th Cav.	12/09/1872
Jordan Hawkins	Pvt.	9th Cav.	12/22/1872
Edward MacComb	AA Surgeon		1/14/1873
Henry Warren	Pvt.	24th Inf.	3/21/1873

James Fox	Pvt.	4th Cav.	1/16/1874
Reuben Britton	Pvt.	24th Inf.	5/18/1874
Robert Wakee	Pvt.	25th Inf.	6/15/1874
Frank Hall	Pvt.	4th Cav.	6/06/1874
Sandy Anderson		24th Inf.	11/08/1874
Cornelius Hooper	Pvt.	4th Cav.	12/12/1874
Issac Blackwell	Pvt.	24th Inf.	5/04/1876
Geo. Schuhriman	Pvt.	8th Cav.	9/12/1876
Michael Schultz	Pvt.	8th Cav.	10/11/1876
Frank Sinclair	Pvt.	8th Cav.	12/05/1876
John Brown	Pvt.	10th Cav.	5/02/1878
Anthony Pitts	Pvt.	24th Inf.	5/28/1878
Thomas Hume	Hosp.	St. USA	8/02/1878
Ernest Strickman	Corp.	10th Cav.	8/02/1878
Robert Bidley		24th Inf.	9/21/1878
E. Dodt	1st Lt. Adj.	24th Inf.	1/05/1879
Daniel Martin	Pvt.	24th Inf.	8/27/1879
Lafayette Harris	Corp.	24th Inf.	9/20/1879
Richard Brown	Pvt.	8th Cav.	9/22/1880
Reuben Stoller	Pvt.	22 Inf.	7/13/1882
Michael Massaro	Pvt.	3rd Cav.	4/10/1891
Burt King	Pvt.	1st Inf.	?

33 others were listed as unknown.

Appendix C

Fort Duncan, Texas, Known as Camp near Eagle Pass
from March 1849 to November 1849;
Fort Duncan from October 1849 to August 9, 1883

LIST OF COMMANDING OFFICERS

Capt. Sidney Burbank, 1st Inf.	3/27/49 to	6/12/49
Capt. John M. Scott, 1st Inf.	6/12/49 to	3/13/50
Maj. Thompson Morris, 1st Inf.	3/13/50 to	7/01/51
Lt. Col. Henry Wilson, 1st Inf.	7/01/51 to	8/06/51
Maj. Morris	8/06/51 to	1/01/54
Capt. Benjamin H. Cuttner, 1st In.	4/20/52 to	6/06/52
Capt. Arthur	4/28/53 to	5/27/53
Col. Joseph Plympton, 1st Inf.	1/01/54 to	4/03/55
Capt. Wm. E. Prince, 1st Inf.	4/06/54 to	5/19/54

Lt. Col. Henry Bainbridge, 1st Inf.   4/03/55 to   7/11/55
Maj. Thompson Morris   5/13/55 to   6/17/55
Capt. George W. Wallace, 1st Inf.   7/11/55 to   8/04/55
Capt. Sidney Burbank, 1st Inf.   8/04/55 to   3/27/56
Capt. G.W. Wallace, 1st Inf.   3/27/56 to 12/29/56
1st Lt. James W. Robinson, 1st Inf.   4/19/56 to   4/21/56
Capt. Thomas Claiborne, R.M.R.   4/21/56 to   5/09/56
Capt. Andrew Porter, R.M.R.   5/09/56 to   7/07/56
Maj. Sidney Burbank, 1st Inf.   12/29/56 to   1/10/59
Capt. Charles C. Gilbert, 1st Inf.   5/15/58 to   6/06/58
Lt. Col. Gouverneur Morris, 1st Inf.   1/10/59 to   5/29/59
Maj. Samuel P. Heintzelman, 1st Inf.   5/29/59 to   6/11/59

Post Abandoned June 11, 1859

Post Reoccupied March 18, 1860
1st Lt. Henry W. Closson, 1st Arty.   3/18/60 to   8/01/60
Capt. William H. French, 1st Arty.   8/01/60 to   1/27/61
1st Lt. James W. Robinson, 1st Arty.   1/27/61 to   2/21/61
Capt. Oliver L. Shepherd, 3rd Inf.   2/21/61 to   3/20/61

Post evacuated March 20, 1861

Capt. F.M. Crandal, 41st Inf.   3/28/68 to   4/01/68
Lt. Col. W.R. Shafter, 41st Inf.   4/01/68 to   4/ /69
Capt. George B. Hoge, 41st Inf.   4/ /69 to 10/25/69
Capt. Jacob C. DeGress, 9th Cav.   10/23/69 to 12/05/69
1st Lt. Edwin A. Bigg, 25th Inf.   12/05/69 to   1/12/70
Capt. Jacob C. DeGress, 9th Cav.   1/12/70 to   3/12/70
Capt. Frank W. Perry, 24th Inf.   3/20/70 to   8/17/70
1st Lt. Edwin A. Bigg, 25th Inf.   6/11/70 to   7/05/70
Capt. David Schooley, 25th Inf.   7/05/70 to   8/ /70
Maj. Zenas R. Bliss, 25th Inf.   8/17/70 to 12/16/70
Capt. Frank W. Perry, 24th Inf.   12/16/70 to   1/20/71
Maj. Z.R. Bliss, 25th Inf.   1/20/71 to   4/05/72
Capt. Gaines Lawson, 25th Inf.   5/29/71 to   6/30/71
Capt. David Schooley, 25th Inf.   9/17/71 to 10/02/71
Maj. Henry C. Merriam, 24th Inf.   4/05/72 to 12/03/72
Lt. Col. Wm. R. Shafter, 24th Inf.   12/03/72 to 12/14/76
Capt. Charles C. Hood, 24th Inf.   2/17/73 to   3/13/76
Maj. A.E. Latimer, 4th Cav.   11/13/73 to   2/10/74
Capt. J.W. French, 25th Inf.   5/03/73 to   5/06/74

Capt. C.N.V. Cunningham, 24th Inf.	5/06/74 to 5/21/74
Capt. Cunningham	6/28/74 to 7/07/74
Capt. French	7/07/74 to 2/14/75
Capt. Cunningham	5/25/75 to 6/02/75
Capt. Chas. Parker, 9th Cav.	6/12/75 to 7/14/75
Capt. Wm. L. Kellogg, 10th Inf.	7/14/75 to 12/30/75
Capt. Cunningham	2/22/76 to 3/04/76
Capt. Cunningham	4/10/76 to 5/21/76
Capt. C.A. Hartwell, 8th Cav.	9/26/76 to 5/29/76
Capt. Kellogg	5/29/76 to 8/07/76
Capt. Hartwell, 8th Cav.	8/07/76 to 10/19/76
1st Lt. John D. Stevenson, 8th Cav.	9/26/76 to 10/17/76
Capt. Charles C. Hood, 24th Inf.	12/15/76 to 1/17/77
Maj. G.W. Schofield, 10th Cav.	1/17/77 to 2/11/78
Capt. Hood	3/14/77 to 4/01/77
Lt. Col. Wm. R. Shafter, 24th. Inf.	2/11/78 to 7/23/79
Capt. T.R.P. Hampson, 10th Inf.	7/16/78 to 8/30/78
Capt. Hood	8/30/78 to 10/27/78
Capt. Hood	12/01/78 to 1/28/79
Capt. Frederick M. Crandal, 24th Inf.	1/28/79 to 2/04/79
Capt. Hood	2/04/78 to 3/17/79
Capt. Crandal	3/17/79 to 4/03/79
Capt. Hood	5/05/79 to 7/23/79
Lt. Col. John E. Yard, 24th Inf.	7/23/79 to 4/28/80
Capt. E.B. Williston, 2nd Arty.	10/17/79 to 11/01/79
Capt. Hood	2/18/80 to 3/05/80
Lt. Col. Lewis C. Hunt, 20th Inf.	4/28/80 to 8/26/80
Capt. John S. McNaught, 20th Inf.	8/26/80 to 9/26/80
Capt. Almond B. Wells, 8th Cav.	9/26/80 to 10/03/80
Lt. Col. A.J. Dallas, 22nd Inf.	10/03/80 to 12/14/82
Capt. Platt M. Thorne, 22nd Inf.	7/24/81 to 9/30/81
Capt. H.J. Farnsworth, 8th Cav.	10/19/81 to 12/14/82
Lt. Col. Zenas R. Bliss, 19th Inf.	12/14/82 to 8/21/85
Capt. Jacob H. Smith, 19th Inf.	5/26/83 to 6/15/83
Capt. R.N. Pennington, 19th Inf.	7/25/83 to 8/09/83

Appendix D

OFFICERS PRESENT OR ACCOUNTED FOR
1914

1st Commanding Officer
2d Staff Corps; 3d,
Field and Staff of
Regiment; 4th, Company
Officers, according to rank

No.	Rank.	Regiment or Corps	Company
1. Thomas W. Griffith	Lt Col	19"Inf.	Commanding 17th since March 21/14
2. William P. Banta	Capt	M.C.	Duty with 17th Inf.
3. Philip B. Connolly	1st Lt	M.C.	Duty with 17th Inf.
4. James A. Simpson	1st Lt	M.R.C.	Duty with 17th Inf.
5. George W. Martin	Major	17" Inf	Comdg. 1st Bn. S.
6. Robert Alexander	Major	17" Inf	Comdg. 3rd Bn. S.
7. Benjamin F. Hardaway	Major	17" Inf	Comdg. 2d Bn. S.
8. Henry M. Bankhead	Capt & Adjt	17" Inf	Duty Adjt., Camp Commanding N.C.S. & B.
9. Charles B. Stone, Jr.	Capt & Comsy	17" Inf	Duty, Actg. R.Q.M.
10. Henry L. Durrant	Chapln	17" Inf	Duty
11. William H. Clendenin	1 Lt & B.A.	17" Inf	Duty, Exchange Off.
12. Thorne Strayer	1 Lt & B.A.	17" Inf	Duty, Comdg. Reg.
13. Frederick W. Boschen	1 Lt & B.A.	17" Inf	Duty
14. Ralph E. Jones	2d Lt BQM & C	17" Inf	Duty, Asst to Cap.
15. Clarence M. McMurray	2d Lt BQM & C	17"Inf	Duty, Asst. to Cap.
16. Durwood S. Wilson	2d Lt BQM & C	17"Inf	Duty, Comdg, M.G.
17. Benjamin T. Simmons	Capt	17" Inf B	Comdg. Company
18. Percy M. Cochran	Capt	17" Inf E	Comdg. Company
19. Henry S. Wagner	Capt	17" Inf A	Comdg. Co. since April SO 54 WD Apr 22/14; Apr 24/14, joined same
20. James S. Young, Jr.	Capt	17" Inf M	Comdg. Co.
21. John W. Wright	Capt	17" Inf D	Comdg. Co. Intelligence Camp Eagle Pass, Texas

22. Jack Hayes	Capt	17" Inf F	Comdg. Company
23. Horace P. Hobbs	Capt	17" Inf G	Comdg. Co. Joined from turn for Mar. 1914, SK.
24. Paul W. Beck	Capt	17" Inf L	Comdg. Co.
25. Oliver F. Snyder	Capt	17" Inf H	Comdg. Co. Promoted SO 80 WD Apr 6/14, As 11/14.
26. H. Clay M. Supplee	1"Lt.	17" Inf G	With Co. Reg. Ord. Sig. Officer, per RSO
27. Daniel M. Cheston, Jr.	1"Lt	17" Inf D	With Co. Att. to & Co.
28. Thomas C. Musgrave	1"Lt	17" Inf E	With Co.
29. Charles F. Severson	1"Lt	17" Inf F	With Co. Police Off.
30. John D. Burnett	1"Lt	17" Inf B	Att to & Comdg. Co. K 65 1914. Duty with Co.
31. Earl C. Buck	1"Lt	17" Inf I	Comdg. Co
32. Arthur C. Evans	2"Lt	17" Inf D	With Co.
33. John E. Creed	2"Lt	17" Inf B	With Co.
34. John H. Harrison	2"Lt	17" Inf C	With Co.
35. Ralph S. Kimball	2"Lt	17" Inf H	With Co.
36. Paul X. English	2"Lt	17" Inf F	With Co.
37. Roland F. Walsh	2"Lt	17" Inf L	With Co.

Appendix E

OFFICERS PRESENT OR ACCOUNTED FOR
November 1915

NAME	RANK	UNIT	COMP
1. Henry C. Hodges, Jr.	Col	17th Inf.	C
2. Thomas S. Bratton	Major	Med Corps	S
3. Horace M. Roberson	Capt	Med Corps	T SD
4. Robert Alexander	Major	17th Inf	C
5. George C. Saffarrans	Major	17th Inf	C
6. Benjamin F. Hardaway	Major	17th Inf	C
7. John L. Maddox	Chap	17th Inf	C

8. Percy M. Cochran	Capt	17th Inf	QM	C
9. Thorne Strayer	1st Lt	17th Inf	BA	C
10. Ralph S. Kimball	2nd Lt	17th Inf	BQMC	A
11. Bryan Conrad	Capt	17th Inf	G	C
12. Henry S. Wagner	Capt	17th Inf	A	C
13. James S. Young, Jr.	Capt	17th Inf	M	C
14. John W. Wright	Capt	17th Inf	D	C
				Ad
15. Frederick Goedecke	Capt	17th Inf	H	C
16. Robert C. Humber	Capt	17th Inf	B	C
17. John B. W. Corey	Capt	6 F A F		C
18. James G. Taylor	Capt	17th Inf	F	C
19. Charles A. Thuis	1st Lt	17th Inf	C	C
20. Thomas C. Musgrave	1st Lt	17th Inf	L	C
21. Roderick Dew	1st Lt	17th Inf	K	C
22. Merrill E. Spalding	1st Lt	17th Inf	F	I
23. Lucien H. Taliaferro	2nd Lt	6 F A F		I
24. Whitmon R. Conolly	2nd Lt	17th Inf	H	I
25. Floyd D. Carlock	2nd Lt	17th Inf	D	I
26. Frank B. Clay	2nd Lt	17th Inf	C	I
				S
27. Hugh B. Keen	2nd Lt	17th Inf	G	
28. Leland S. Devore	2nd Lt	17th Inf	M	
29. Ernst Sedlacek	2nd Lt	6 F A	F	
30. George P. Nickerson	2nd Lt	17th Inf	A	
31. J. Warren Weissheimer	2nd Lt	17th Inf	I	
32. Howard Donelly	2nd Lt	17th Inf	B	
33. Vernon E. Prichard	2nd Lt	17th Inf	L	
34. Gilbert S. Brownell	2nd Lt	17th Inf	E	
35. Robert L. Williams Add	2nd Lt	17th Inf	F	

ABSENT

George B. Duncan	Lt Col	17th Inf
Fred L. Walker	2nd Lt	17th Inf
Edward S. Walton	Capt	17th Inf
Alexander M. Wetherill	Capt	17th Inf

Appendix 7

WAR DEPARTMENT
The Adjutant General's Office
Washington

LIST OF THE COMMANDING OFFICERS
OF CAMP EAGLE PASS, TEXAS

Capt. William H. McLaughlin, 18th Inf. Jan. 20, 1892 Apr. 8, 1892
Maj. Henry W. Wessells, Jr., 3rd Cav. Apr. 8, 1892 June 9, 1893
Capt. George A. Drew, 3rd Cav. Oct. 22, 1892 Feb. 7, 1893
2nd Lt. William F. Grote, 18th Inf. June 9, 1893 June 20, 1893
Capt. George H. Paddock, 5th Cav. June 20, 1893 May 21, 1894
Capt. Winfield S. Edgerly, 7th Cav. May 21, 1894 Nov. 15, 1894
Capt. C. H. Watts, 5th Cav. Nov. 15, 1894 May 13, 1895
Capt. George H. Paddock, 5th Cav. May 13, 1895 Dec. 13, 1895
Capt. Lea Febiger, 23rd Inf. Dec. 13, 1895 Apr. 16, 1896
Lt. Benjamin C. Morse, 23rd Inf. May 24, 1897 June 21, 1897
1st Lt. Benjamin C. Morse, 23rd Inf. Apr. 16, 1898 May 25, 1898
1st Lt. Chas. H. Moody, 3rd Texas May 25, 1898 July 15, 1898
    Vol. Inf.
1st Lt. John L. Sparger, 3rd Texas July 15, 1898 Sept 24, 1898
    Vol. Inf.
Maj. Alfred W. Drew, 3rd Texas Sept 24, 1898 Dec. 23, 1898
    Vol. Inf.
Capt. Edmond G. Shields, 3rd Texas Dec. 23, 1898 Feb. 16, 1899
    Vol. Inf.
2nd Lt. Henry C. Whitehead, 10th Cav. Feb. 17, 1899 May —, 1899
Astg. Asst. Surg. Malone Duggan, July 22, 1899 Aug. 28, 1899
Astg. Asst. Surg. Malone Duggan, Sept 4, 1899 Oct. 27, 1899
2nd Lt. Thomas A. Roberts, 10th Cav. Feb. 5, 1900 July 7, 1900

From July 9, 1900 to February 15, 1902, the post was a sub-post, under the command of the Commanding Officer of Fort Clark, Texas. During this period, the following officers were in command of the detachment at Camp Eagle Pass.

Capt. Robert D. Reed, Jr., 10th Cav. July 7, 1900 Mar. 31, 1901

Capt. W. C. Rafferty, Arty. Corps. Mar. 31, 1901 Oct. 16, 1901
2nd Lt. Edward M. Offley, 12th Cav. Oct. 17, 1901 Feb. 15, 1902
1st Lt. Halstead Dorey, 4th Inf. Feb. 15, 1902 May 28, 1902
2nd Lt. Fred L. Davidson, 4th Inf. May 28, 1902 June 24, 1902
2nd Lt. Robert M. Beck, 12th Cav. June 25, 1902 July 3, 1902
Capt. Ernesto V. Smith, 4th Inf. July 3, 1902 May 1903
Lt. Lewis Case, 12th Cav Nov. 30, 1902 Dec. 12, 1902
Capt. James Clinton, 18th Inf May 20, 1903 Oct. 28. 1903
Lt. James T. Watson, 26th Inf. Oct. 28, 1903 Dec. 9, 1903
Lt. Robert K. Spiller, 26th Inf Dec 9, 1903 Feb. 29, 1904
2nd Lt. Albert T Rich, 26th Inf. Feb. 29 1904 Mar 2, 1904
Lt. Robert K. Spiller, 26th Inf. Mar 2, 1904 Apr —, 1904

Appendix G

THE ADJUTANT GENERAL'S OFFICE
Washington

List of the Commanding Officers of the Eagle Pass District, Texas

Brig. Gen. Henry A. Greene, U.S. Army May 23, 1916 Aug. —, 1916
Brig. Gen. Frederick W. Sibley, U.S. Army Aug. 26, 1916 Oct. 17, 1916
Col. E. A. Miller, 3rd F.A. Oct. 17, 1916 Nov. 4, 1916
Col. E. A. Miller, 3rd F.A. Nov. 5, 1916 Nov. 21, 1916
Col. E. A. Miller, 3rd F.A. Dec. 5, 1916 Dec. 20, 1916
Brig. Gen. Francis H. French, U.S. Army Dec. 31, 1916 Jan. 1, 1917
Brig. Gen. James Parker, U.S. Army Apr. 19, 1917 May 11, 1917 (1st Prov. Div.)
Col. R. L. Hirst, 3rd Inf. May —, 1917 May —, 1917
Lt. Col. George E. Lovell, 14th Cav. Nov. 18, 1917 Dec. 13, 1917
Col. Frederick R. Day, 3rd Inf. Dec. 14, 1917 Dec. 26, 1917
Col. Augustus C. Macomb, 14th Cav. Dec. 27, 1917 Jan. 30, 1918
Col. Frederick R. Day, 3rd Inf. Jan. 31, 1918 Feb. 16, 1918
Col. Augustus C. Macomb, 14th Cav. Feb. 16, 1918 Mar. 31, 1918
Col. Frederick R. Day, 3rd Inf. Apr. 1, 1918 June 20, 1918
Col. Ervin L. Phillips, 307th Cav. June 20, 1918 July —, 1918
Lt. Col. Sheldon W. Anding, attached July —, 1918 Nov. 5, 1918 3rd Inf.
Col. Gustav A. Wieser, 3rd Inf. Nov. 5, 1918 Dec. —, 1919
Col. Paul Giddings, 3rd Inf. Dec. 21, 1919 Apr. 28, 1920
Col. Sedgwick Rice, Apr. 11, 192() Apr. 28, 192()

Col. Giddings, Apr. 28, 1920 Oct. 10, 1920
Col. James H. Bradford, Jr., 46th Inf. Oct. 10, 1920 Dec. 31, 1920

Appendix H

COMMANDING OFFICERS
Camp Eagle Pass, Texas

Lt. Col. Thomas W. Griffith, 19th Inf. Mar. 21, 1914 Apr. 6, 1914
Col. Thomas W. Griffith, 17th Inf. Apr. 6, 1914 July 16, 1914
Maj. Robert Alexander, 17th Inf. July 29, 1914 Oct. 1, 1914
Lt. Col. Henry C. Hale, 17th Inf. Oct. 1, 1914 Nov. 20, 1914
Col. Henry C. Hodges, Jr., 17th lnf. Nov. 21, 1914 Feb. 23, 1916
Maj. Robert Alexander, 17th Inf. Feb. 23, 1916 Apr. 19, 1916
Maj. Samuel Burkhardt, 19th Inf. Apr. 20, 1916 May 16,
Lt. Col. Julius A. Penn, 3rd Inf. May 16, 1916 July 5, 1916
Col. Edwin A. Root, 30th Inf. July 5, 1916 Aug. 25, 1916
Col. Robert L. Hirst, 3rd Inf. Aug. 26, 1916 July 20, 1917
Lt. Col. Robert C. Williams, attached 3rd Inf. July 21, 1917 July 28, 1917
Col. Robert L. Hirst, 3rd Inf. July 28, 1917 Aug. 20, 1917
Lt. Col. Robert C. Williams, attached 3rd Inf. Aug. 24, 1917 Sept. 6, 1917
Lt. Col. Robert C. Williams, attached 3rd Inf. Sep. 10, 1917 Oct. 5, 1917
Maj. Paul Giddings, attached 3rd Inf. Oct. 6, 1917 Oct. 6, 1917
Lt. Col. Robert C. Williams, attached 3rd Inf. Oct. 9, 1917 Oct. 11, 1917
Maj. George E. Lovell, 14th Cav. Oct. —, 1917 Nov. 16, 1917
Maj. Harry E. Comstock, 3rd Inf. Nov. 15, 1917 Dec. 13, 1917
Col. Frederick R. Day, 3rd Inf. Dec. 14, 1917 Feb. 17, 1918
Maj. Edward C. Wells, 14th Cav. Feb. 18, 1918 Mar. 8, 1918
Col. Frederick R. Day, 3rd Inf. Mar. 9, 1918 June 20, 1918
Maj. William J. Connelly, 3rd Inf. June 20, 1918 June 25, 1918
Lt. Col. Sheldon W. Anding, attached 3rd Inf. June 25, 1918 Nov. —, 1918
Col. Gustav A. Wieser, 3rd Inf. Nov. —, 1918 Dec. —, 1919
Col. Paul Giddings, 3rd Inf. Dec. 21, 1919 June —, 1920
Lt. Col. Paul Giddings 3rd Ind. June —, 1920 Oct. 10, 1920
Col. James H. Bradford, 44th Inf. Oct. 10, 1920 Nov. 15, 1921
Maj. Frederick M. Armstrong, 46th Inf. June 4, 1921 June 22, 1921
Lt. Col. William S. Sinclair, 46th Inf. Aug. 2, 1921 Aug. 9, 1921
Capt. Andrew J. Wynne, Cav. Nov. 15, 1921 Dec. —, 1921
Capt. D. B. Culliname, Cav. Dec. —, 1921 Mar.4, 1922

Appendix 7

Official Roster, 1st Kansas Infantry
(In United States Service)
Headquarters and entire regiment at Eagle Pass, Texas 1916

Col. Wilder S. Metcalf
Lt. Col. Charles S. Flanders
Maj. Frank W. Butler, commanding 2nd Battalion
Maj. Aaron K. Hitchens, commanding 3rd Battalion
Maj. Hugh Means, commanding 1st Battalion
Capt. Samuel G. Fairchild, Regimental Adjutant
Capt. Lute P. Stovar, Regimental Inspector of small arms
Capt. James Naismith, Regimental Chaplain
1st Lt. William L. Stryker, Adjutant 3rd Battalion
1st Lt. Miles E. Canty, Adjutant 2nd Battalion
1st Lt. John A. Ashworth, Adjutant 1st Battalion

Machine-gun Company, Humboldt—Capt. Albert H. Krause, commanding; 1st Lt. Leigh Hunt, 2nd Lt. Charles H. Browne, 2nd Lt. Frank D. Matthias

Supply Company, Lawrence—Capt. Frank L. Travis, 2nd Lt. Darley S. James

Company A, Kansas City—Capt. Archie K. Rupert, 1st Lt. Wyndham A. Simpson, 2nd Lt. William A. Firstenberger

Company B, Horton—Capt. John R. Thompson, 1st Lt. Andrew Thompson, 2nd Lt. Albert O. Bradshaw

Company C, Burlington—Capt. Frank Farmley, 1st Lt. Wilbur T. Pharee, 2nd Lt. William C. Flock

Company D, Paola—Capt. George J. Frank, 1st Lt. Robert S. Ayers, 2nd Lt. John B. Salisbury

Company E, Fredonia—1st Lt. Bruce E. Stryker, 2nd Lt. Fritz W. Koch

Company F, Hiawatha—Capt. Henry J. Weltmer, 1st Lt. Oscar O. Hauber, 2nd Lt. Albert S. Bigelow

Company G, Fort Scott—Capt. John H. Prichard, 1st Lt. Harry A. Cooper, 2nd Lt. Charles R. Fisher

Company H, Lawrence—Capt. Samuel G. Clark, 1st Lt. Guy N. Walling, 2nd Lt. Oscar C. Brownlee

Company I, Manhattan—Capt. Willis L. Pearce, 1st Lt. Arthur Scheleen, 2nd Lt. C.R. Keller

Company K, Garnett—Capt. Floyd E. Potter, 1st Lt. Lewis C. McDonald, 2nd Lt. Frank O. Gillette

Company L, Yates Center—Capt. Earl T. Patterson, 1st Lt. Paul A. Cannady, 2nd Lt. George L. Hunt

Company M, Lawrence—Capt. Frank E. Jones, 1st Lt. Edward M. Briggs, 2nd Lt. Lester A. Sprinkle

Sanitary Troops—Maj. Henry T. Salisburgy, Capt. Seth A. Hammel, Capt. Irn E. Durant, 1st Lt. Joseph S. Alford

Appendix J
OPERATIONS FLIGHT MANUAL
CURTISS AEROPLANE CO. 1911

Rules Governing the Use of the Curtiss Aeronautical Apparatus:

1. The aeronaut should seat himself in the apparatus, and secure himself firmly to the chair by means of the strap provided. On the attendant crying "Contest!" the aeronaut should close the switch which supplies electrical current to the motor, thus enabling the attendant to set the same in motion.

2. Opening the control valve of the motor, the aeronaut should at the same time firmly grasp the vertical stick or control pole which is to be found directly before the chair. The power from the motor will cause the device to roll gently forward, then the aeronaut should govern its direction of motion by use of the rudder bars.

3. When the mechanism is facing into the wind, the aeronaut should open the control valve of the motor to its fullest extent, at the same time pulling the control pole gently toward his (the aeronaut's) middle anatomy.

4. When sufficient speed has been attained, the device will leave the ground and assume the position of aeronautical ascent.

5. Should the aeronaut decide to return to terra-firma, he should close the control valve of the motor. This will cause the apparatus to assume what is known as the "gliding position," except in the case of these flying machines which are inherently unstable. These latter will assume the position known as "involuntary spin" and will return to earth without further action on the part of the aeronaut.

6. On approaching closely to the chosen field or terrain, the aeronaut should move the control pole gently toward himself, thus causing the machine to alight more or less gently on terra-firma.

(Verbatim reprint of operations sheet issued by Curtiss for their 1911 "Pusher Aeroplane.")

Appendix K

Eagle Pass Reflections by Oscar Horak

Oscar entered the U.S. Army as member of 17th Regiment of Infantry July 18, 1914. Discharged November 20, 1916. His mother requested a hardship discharge due to his father's death. Oscar was disappointed at not finishing his army enlistment and consequently joined the navy later, in June of 1917.

• Traveled to Eagle Pass by train from Columbus, Ohio, and met rest of his unit who were returning from the Philippines.

• His unit consisted of Infantry, mounted calvery Artillery, and a 2-Beater airplane ("for scouting").

• After serving several months as a soldier (going on patrols, digging trenches in case of battles, and helping on KP duty), he was promoted to Cook 1st Class.

• He cooked on large wood cook stoves, and built their own dutch ovens for baking. "I could make 48 pancakes at once," he recalled. Oscar cooked for his company of 65 men.

• Meals were beef, beans, potatoes, rice, gravy, eggs and whatever vegetables were available.

• Oscar and another soldier would sometimes get a 2-day duty excuse to go hunting—by horse and wagon—for jack rabbits and quail for camp meals.

• Oscar was popular in his company for his inventive dishes, one of which was made using hardtack — dry pressed biscuit—that were unpopular with the soldiers. But he made a baked dish out of it with layers of tomatoes and sugar that was so good he'd go around to the other companies to collect their unwanted hardtack.

• Another time, Oscar recalled arriving a bit too late one morning to prepare a proper breakfast (he'd stayed up all night playing poker) so he used leftover potatoes from the previous night's supper, mixed ham with some onions and eggs and baked it all together. Pershing liked it so much he asked Oscar, "What do you call this dish?" To which Oscar quickly replied, "Potato Omlette!"

• Oscar often had officers in the mess tent, around the tables, drinking coffee, and he recalls chatting often with Pershing himself. He once asked Pershing why he always kept an unlit cigarette in his mouth. Pershing replied, "I like a cool smoke."

• Oscar remembers that although their unit had a big recreation tent for pool, poker and other games, many of the men would sneak across the river at night to visit the cantinas and casinos in town. They couldn't be seen in their uniforms, so they would keep a set of (shared) civilian clothes at the bars and change when they arrived. A chance to dance with the cantina girls was just too enticing.

• Oscar remembers Pershing as an extremely strict, disciplined man who expected excellent service from his men, especially his officers; but he also had a high regard and sense of responsibility to his soldiers. Oscar said he often heard Pershing verbally and loudly reprimand an officer or soldier for misconduct. He once witnessed an angry Pershing reprimand and demote one of his officers because the officer had refused to get medical attention for a soldier with badly blistered feet on their march into Mexico.

• Oscar was once ordered to accompany a black soldier (convicted of murdering a fellow soldier during an argument), to El Paso, Texas, for transporting on to Leavenworth Prison. He was given instructions that he would serve the soldier's sentence if he let him escape—so Oscar was prepared to use his revolver if necessary. But he told the fellow that Leavenworth was overloaded now and they'd probably discharge him early. So there were no problems. The prisoner "behaved himself good," Oscar recalled.

• Oscar once remembers diving into the river near Piedras Negras after hearing shooting, only to discover that the townsfolk were celebrating the election of Carranza (defeating Pancho Villa) with fireworks and shooting.

• Although Oscar never saw battles on his marches and patrols into Mexico, their patrols were not without tension and apprehension. He recalls that one night an over-anxious patrol guard shot and killed an advancing—cow!

(NOTE: References to General Pershing and Mexico occurred during Punitive Expedition by American Regular Army troops in 1916.)

Notes

Chapter 1

1. Webb, *Handbook of Texas,* 2:835; Field, "Texas Military History Fort Duncan," Vol. 2, 1967, pg. 161: Texas A & M, "Maverick County, Long Range Program," pg. 14.

2. Webb, *Handbook,* op. cit., *Lamar Papers, IV,* pg. 198-199.

3. C. G. Downing, "100 Years Relatively Speaking," *Eagle Pass News Guide,* September 16, 1971. Little known facts regarding Fort Duncan.

4. Webb, *Handbook,* op. cit.

5. Field, "Texas Military History," op. cit.

6. Ben E. Pingenot, *Paso Del Aguila,* 26, 39-40.

7. Senate Exec. Doc. No. 52, "The Treaty Between United States and Mexico—1848."

8. Ibid.

9. Ibid.

10. Ibid.

11. A. B. Bender, "The Texas Frontier," *SWHQ,* 37:127-135. "Sharps Rifles and Spanish Mules."

12. Roy E. Graham, "Federal Fort Architecture in Texas." *SWHQ,* 74: 167.

13. Ibid.

14. Ibid.

15. Parmenus Turnley, *Reminiscences,* 115.

16. National Archives, "Returns U.S. Military Posts, 1800-1916, M616, Roll #335."

17. Ibid.

18. Francis B. Heitman, *Historical Register and Dictionary of the United States Army,* vol. 2.

19. *Register of Graduates, USMA*, 1980 Edition.
20. National Archives, op. cit.
21. Heitman, "Historical Register," op. cit.
22. Ibid.
23. *Register, USMA*, op. cit.
24. Heitman, *Historical Register*, op. cit.
25. *Register, USMA*, op. cit.
26. National Archives, op. cit.
27. Ibid.
28. Ibid.
29. Ibid.
30. Ibid.
31. Ibid.
32. Heitman, "Historical Register," op. cit.
33. *Register, USMA*, op. cit.
34. National Archives, op. cit.
35. Letters rec'd. Mrs. Turner, 1909. Regarding Col. Duncan's belongings at USMA. Copy in author's possession.
36. Turnley, *Reminiscences*, op. cit.
37. National Archives, op. cit.
38. Ibid.
39. Ibid.
40. Ibid.
41. Ibid.
42. Kenneth Neighbors, *Indian Exodus*, 74.
43. Ibid.
44. Heitman, *Historical Register*, op. cit.
45. Senate Exec. Doc. No. 64, "Report of Captain W.H.C. Whiting on Inspection of Fort Duncan and Surrounding Area-March 14, 1850."
46. National Archives, op. cit.
47. Ibid.
48. Ibid.
49. G.B.W. Evans, *Mexican Gold Trail*, 61.
50. Ibid.
51. National Archives, op. cit.
52. Ibid.
53. Bexar County Census, 1850.
54. National Archives, op. cit.
55. Ibid.
56. Ibid.
57. Ibid.
58. Ibid.
59. Heitman, *Historical Register*, op. cit.
60. Kenneth Wiggins Porter, *The Negro on the American Frontier*, 437.
61. Ibid.
62. William L. Katz, *Black Indians: A Hidden Heritage*, 77-83.

63. Ibid.
64. National Archives, op. cit.
65. Ibid.
66. Ibid.
67. Ibid.
68. Ibid.
69. Ibid.
70. Kenneth Porter, *Negro on the American Frontier,* op. cit.
71. National Archives, op. cit. Heitman, *Historical Register,* op. cit.
72. National Archives, op. cit.
73. Heitman, *Historical Register,* op. cit.
74. National Archives, op. cit.
75. Ibid.
76. Center for American History, Univ. of Texas, Austin, "Fort Duncan Files, Misc."
77. Webb, *Handbook,* 2:813.
78. Center for American History, op. cit., "Crimmons Papers and Ft. Duncan Files"; *SWHQ,* 52:444-447.
79. Ibid.
80. National Archives, op. cit.
81. Ibid.
82. Ibid.
83. P. H. Sheridan, *Personal Memoirs,* 5 vols., Center for American History, Univ. of Texas, Austin.
84. Ibid.
85. National Archives, op. cit.
86. Ibid.
87. Sheridan, *Memoirs,* op. cit.
88. National Archives, op. cit.
89. Zenas R. Bliss, "Unpublished Memoirs," 5 vols., Center for American History, Univ. of Texas, Austin.
90. Richard Johnson, *A Soldier's Reminiscences in Peace and War,* 61-65.
91. Ibid.
92. Ibid.
93. National Archives, op. cit.
94. Letters Rec'd. D. Duncan to Author, 1988. Regarding unknown camp NE of Eagle Pass.
95. National Archives, op. cit.
96. Ibid.
97. Heitman, *Historical Register,* op. cit.
98. National Archives, op. cit.
99. Ibid.
100. Ibid.
101. Sheridan, *Memoirs,* op. cit.
102. National Archives, op. cit.
103. Ernest Shearer, "The Callahan Expedition-1855," *SWHO* 54:436-449.

104. Ibid.

105. Ibid.

106. K. Porter, *Negro American Frontier,* op. cit.

107. Shearer, "Callahan," op. cit.

108. Maj. W. Emory, "U.S. Mexican Boundary Survey," Vol. 1.

109. Ibid.

110. Ibid.

111. Ibid.

112. National Archives, op. cit.

113. Ibid.; Heitman, *Historical Register,* op. cit.

114. A. B. Bender, "Col. J.F.K. Mansfield Inspection of the Department of Texas- 1856," *SWHO*, Vol. 38.

115. Ibid.

116. Ibid.

117. Ibid.

118. National Archives, op. cit.

119. Commemorative Plaque erected by State of Texas, 1936: National Archives, op. cit.

120. National Archives, op. cit.

121. Webb, *Handbook,* op. cit.

122. Ibid. Jack Lafferty, "La Espanola helped make Eagle Pass safe place," *San Antonio Express-News,* November 24, 1957.

123. Lafferty, "La Espanola," op. cit.

124. National Archives, op. cit.

125. Heitman, *Historical Register,* op. cit.

126. National Archives, op. cit.

172. Ibid.

128. Orders and Memoranda, Department of Texas; Book of Orders, The U.S. Army, 1860, Old Army Section, National Archives, Washington, D.C.

129. Heitman, *Historical Register,* op. cit.

130. National Archives, op. cit.

131. Martin L. Crimmons, "Robert E. Lee in Texas," *Frontier Times,* December 1929; Webb, *Handbook*, op. cit.

132. Ibid.

133. Texas State Archives-Austin, Letter, Lee to Houston, Regarding Bandit Cortina.

134. National Archives, op. cit.

135. Bibliography.

136. M. L. Crimmons, Letter to C.F. Hedrick. Regarding Lee in Texas. Copy in author's possession.

137. Texas Archives, Lee letter to Houston, op. cit.

138. National Archives, op. cit.; Center for American History, Fort Duncan Files.

139. Ibid.

140. Ibid.

141. Book of Order, 1860, op. cit.

142. Register, USMA, op. cit.

143. National Archives, op. cit.

144. Heitman, *Historical Register,* op. cit.; Register, USMA, op. cit.

145. National Archives, op. cit.

146. Ibid.

147. Ibid.

148. Ibid.

149. Heitman, *Historical Register,* op. cit.

150. Orders-Dept. of Texas, op. cit.; National Archives, op. cit.

151. National Archives, op. cit.

Chapter 2

1. National Archives, op. cit.

2. Ibid.

3. D. Worrell, "Threat of Knights of Golden Circle," *Eagle Pass News-Guide,* June 28, 1956.

4. Worrell, "Evacuation of Fort Duncan," op. cit., April 30, 1953.

5. Ibid.

6. Worrell, "Threat," op. cit.

7. Webb, *Handbook,* op. cit.

8. National Archives, op. cit.; Center for American History, Fort Duncan Files.

9. Webb, *Handbook,* op. cit., 587.

10. Ibid., 588.

11. Ibid., 351, 651.

12. Ibid., 285.

13. Ibid., 651.

14. Ibid., 283.

15. Ibid., 651-652.

16. Ibid.

17. Ibid., 651; "The War of the Rebellion," Ware's Report to Col. Ford, 1034-5.

18. Webb, *Handbook,* op. cit., 651.

19. War of Rebellion, op. cit., 1034.

20. Ibid.; Pingenot, *Paso del Aguila,* 11.

21. Ibid.

22. "War of Rebellion," op. cit.

23. Neighbors, *Indian Exodus,* op. cit.; A. Gibson, *The Kickapoos: Lords of the Middle Border,* 1963.

24. Ibid.

25. R. Thompson, *Crossing the Border.*

26. Webb, *Handbook,* op. cit., 600-601.

27. R. Sellers, "The History of Fort Duncan-Eagle Pass." Master's thesis, Sul Ross University, 1960.

28. Ibid.

29. Webb, *Handbook,* op. cit.

30. Ibid.

31. Ibid., 469.

Chapter 3

1. Francis Heitman, *Historical Register and Dictionary United States Army 1789-1903.*

2. Ibid.

3. Morris Schaff, "The Spirit of Old West Point," 48-49.

4. Ibid.

5. Special Orders No. 3, Department of Texas, March 23, 1868.

6. Heitman, *Historical Register,* op. cit.

7. Special Orders No. 3, Department of Texas.

8. RG 393, National Archives, Records of U.S. Army Commands. Microfilm Roll #617.

9. Heitman, *Historical Register,* op. cit.

10. Ibid.

11. Microfilm Roll 617, Post Returns; Thompson, *Crossing the Border,* P. Carlson, Ph.D. dissertation, "W.R. Shafter: Military Commander in the American West," Texas Tech University, 1973.

12. Heitman, *Historical Register,* op. cit.

13. Ibid.; Thompson, *Crossing the Border,* op. cit.

14. Heitman, *Historical Register,* op. cit.; T. Cruse, "Apache Days and After"; B. Davis, "The Truth About Geronimo."

15. Ibid.

16. Ibid.

17. Ibid.

18. RG 393 Army Commands.

19. Ibid.

20. Carlson, "Shafter," Ph.D. dissertation.

21. Ibid.

22. RG 393, Army Commands.

23. Ibid.

24. Ibid.

25. Heitman, *Historical Register,* Graduates of U.S. Military Academy.

26. RG 393 Army Commands; Carlson, "Shafter," Ph.D. dissertation.

27. Heitman, *Historical Register*; Carlson, "Shafter," Ph.D. dissertation.

28. Ibid.

29. RG 393 Army Commands.

30. Letter to D. Furrier, New York, 1869. Copy in author's possession.

31. RG 393 Army Commands; Sheridan, *Record of Engagements, 1881.*

32. Ibid.

33. Heitman, *Historical Register*; Carlson, "Shafter," Ph.D. dissertation.

34. Heitman, *Historical Register*; *United States Medal of Honor Recipients*, 3rd ed., 1980.

35. Z. Bliss, "Unpublished Memoirs."

36. Ibid.

37. Ibid.; Thompson, *Crossing the Border;* RG 393 Army Commands.

38. Ibid.

39. Woodhull, "Seminole Indian Scouts," *Frontier Times*, Vol. 15, No. 3, December 1937.

40. Ibid.

41. Bliss, "Unpublished Memoirs."

42. Ibid.

43. RG 393 Army Commands.

44. Ibid.

45. Porter, *SWHQ*, January 1952; Genealogy of Scouts-Letters Recd, SNIS Cemetery Assoc.

46. RG 393 Army Commands.

47. Ibid.; Bliss, "Unpublished Memoirs."

48. Ibid.

49. War Department Quartermaster General's Office, "Outline Description of U.S. Military Posts and Stations in 1871."

50. RG 393 Army Commands.

51. Records General Orders Department of Texas, 1871. National Archives.

52. Ibid.

53. War Dept. General Court Martial orders #29, Adj. Gen. Office, December 20, 1871.

54. Sellers, "History of Fort Duncan," op. cit.; "Colonel Pedro A. Valdes, Una Leyenda Recordada," Coah, Mexico.

55. Ibid.

56. Ibid., RG 393 Army Commands.

57. Ibid.; Bliss, "Unpublished Memoirs."

58. Heitman, *Historical Register,* and RG 393 Army Commands.

59. RG 393 Army Commands.

60. Ibid.

61. Carlson, "William Shafter," RG 393 Army Commands.

62. Thompson, *Crossing the Border*; R. G. Carter, "On the Border With Mackenzie."

63. RG 393 Army Commands

64. Thompson, *Crossing the Border*.

65. Ibid.

66. Senate Exec. Doc. #367, 61st Congress, 2nd Session, 1144-1145; "Protocol of an Agreement Concerning Pursuit of Indians Across the Border."

67. Thompson, *Crossing the Border*; Wallace, *Ranald S. Mackenzie Correspondence 1871-73*.

68. RG 393 Army Commands.

69. Ibid.

70. Ibid.

71. Carlson, "William Shafter."

72. Thompson, *Crossing the Border*; Carter, *On the Border*; Letters Recd, RG 91.

73. Minutes of both House and Senate, sitting at Austin as the 13th Legislature, May 1873.

74. RG 393 Army Commands.

75. Personal examination by the author.
76. RG 393 Army Commands.
77. Porter, "Seminole-Negro Indian Scouts," *SWHQ,* 54:371.
78. RG 393; Carlson, "Wm. Shafter."
79. RG 393 Army Commands.
80. Ibid.; Carlson, "Shafter."
81. Thompson, *Crossing the Border.*
82. RG 393 Army Commands.
83. Ibid.; Carlson, "Wm. Shafter."
84. Ibid.
85. Ibid.; RG 91, Letters Received.
86. Ibid.
87. Thompson, *Crossing the Border*; Carter, *On the Border.*
88. *Requerdos*, Magazine for South Texas School Teachers.
89. RG 393 Army Commands; Carlson, "Wm. Shafter."
90. House Exec. Doc. #13, June 1, 1877, 14-15.
91. RG 393 Army Commands.
92. Ibid.; "Wm Shafter."
93. Ibid.
94. Ibid.
95. Thompson, *Crossing the Border*; Carter, *On the Border.*
96. Ibid.; Carlson, "Wm. Shafter."
97. Ibid.; RG 393 Army Commands.
98. Ibid.
99. Ibid.
100. Ibid.
101. Ibid.
102. Ibid.
103. Ibid.
104. Ibid.
105. Ibid.; Thompson, *Crossing the Border*; Carter, *On the Border.*
106. RG 393 U.S. Army Commands.
107. Ibid.
108. Ibid.
109. Senate Exec. Document #367, 1144-1145.
110. RG 393 U.S. Army Commands; Frederick Palmer, *Tasker R. Bliss-Peacemaker*, Dodd Mead, 1934, pp. 103-119.
111. RG 393 U.S. Army Commands.

Chapter 4
1. RG 393, U.S. Army Commands. Letters Received Department of Texas.
2. Ibid.
3. Ibid.
4. Ibid.
5. Ibid., Audit of Commanding Officers.

6. Ibid.

7. Heitman, *Register and Dictionary U.S. Army.*

8. Sellers, "History of Fort Duncan," master's thesis.

9. RG 393 U.S. Army Commands.

10. Ibid.

11. Ibid.

12. Ibid.; Sellers, "History of Fort Duncan."

13. National Weather Service, Washington, D.C.

14. Sellers, "History of Fort Duncan."

15. Ibid.; Crimmons, "Old Fort Duncan."

16. Report of Sec. of War. 2nd Session, 52nd Congress, Vol. 1, 1892.

17. RG 393 U.S. Army Commands.

18. Letters Received, Department of Texas.

19. Report Secretary of War, 2nd Sess. 52nd Congress, Vol. 1, 1892, 116.

20. Ibid.

21. Ibid.

22. Sellers, "History of Fort Duncan."

23. RG 393 U.S. Army Commands.

24. Ibid.

25. Ibid.

26. Ibid.

27. Virginia Johnson, *Unregimented General*; N. Miles, *Serving the Republic.*

28. RG 393 U.S. Army Commands.

29. F. Remington, *Crooked Trails.*

30. Ibid.

31. Ibid.

32. RG 393 U.S. Army Commands.

33. Ibid.

34. Ibid.

35. Thompson, *Crossing the Border.*

36. Thrapp, *Conquest of Apacheria*; B. Davis, *The Truth about Geronimo.*

37. Heitman, *Dictionary of U.S. Army.*

38. RG 393 U.S. Army Commands.

39. Ibid.

40. Ibid.

Chapter 5

1. RG 393 U.S. Army Commands, Microfilm 617-340.

2. Ibid.; Sellers, "History of Fort Duncan."

3. Ibid.

4. Ibid.

5. Letters Received, Department of the Gulf.

6. RG 393 U.S. Army Commands.

7. Ibid.

8. Ibid.

9. Ibid.

10. Ibid.

11. Ibid.

12. Ibid.; Sellers, "History of Fort Duncan."

13. Ibid.

14. Ibid.

15. Ibid.

16. Ibid.

17. Ibid.; RG 393 U.S. Army Commands

18. RG 393 U.S. Army Commands.

19. Ibid.

20. Ibid.

21. Ibid.

22. Ibid.; Records of Enlistments.

23. Sellers, *History of Fort Duncan*; B. Pingenot, *Dedication of Cavalry Barracks*.

24. Ibid.

25. Sellers, "History of Fort Duncan."

26. Ibid.

27. Ibid.

28. Ibid.

29. Ibid.

30. F. Tompkins, *Chasing Villa*; H. M. Mason, *The Great Pursuit*; Letters Received, "U. S. Army Operations Punitive Expedition—1916," et al.

31. Ibid.; Presidential Order, June 18, 1916.

32. RG 393 U.S. Army Commands.

33. Ibid.

34. Ibid.

35. Sellers, "History of Fort Duncan."

36. RG 393 U.S. Army Commands.

37. Ibid.

38. Ibid.

39. Ibid.

40. Ibid.

Chapter 6

1. U.S. Documents, National Archives, 1921.

2. Letters Rec'd., Military Department of Kansas. Adj. Gen. K.N.G.

3. Letters Rec'd., Sam McKone.

4. Letters Rec'd., Military Department of Tennessee. Adj. Gen. Tenn. N.G.

5. Adj. Gen. Kansas National Guard.

6. A.W.W. Woodcock, *Golden Days,* 1961.

7. Ibid.

8. Adj. Gen. Kansas National Guard.

9. C. Scarborough, "Fort Duncan," *Eagle Pass Daily Guide*, November 1934.

10. Ibid.

11. Ibid.

12. *14th Cavalry Regimental History,* 1925; Sellers, "History of Fort Duncan," 94-95; Webb, *Handbook of Texas,* 496-497; *San Antonio Express-News,* June 23, 1963; Jack Laferty, "Old Fort Duncan Recalls Colorful Texas History."

13. Ibid.

14. Ibid.

15. Ibid.

16. Ibid.

17. Ibid.

18. Ibid.

19. Ibid.

20. Ibid.

21. Recollection of Mr. and Mrs. Charles G. Downing, Fort Clark, Texas, 1989.

22. Letters Recd. Albert F. Simpson Historical Research Center, Maxwell AFB, Alabama.

23. Ibid.

24. Ibid.

25. Personal Letter to E.G. Daughtrey, Del Rio, Texas, April 15, 1982.

26. Simpson Research Center, Maxwell AFB.

27. RG 93, National Archives.

28. Ibid.

29. Sellers, "History of Fort Duncan."

30. Ibid.

31. RG 93, National Archives; Sellers, "History of Fort Duncan."

32. *Eagle Pass News-Guide,* July 1928.

Chapter 7

1. RG 94, National Archives.

2. Ibid.

3. Minutes City Commissioners, Major T.R. Jones, August 4, 1933.

4. Sellers, "History of Fort Duncan," Office of M General, U.S. Army February 25, 1938, "Specifications of Sale for Government-owned land comprising The Eagle Pass Military Reservation, Eagle Pass, Texas."

5. Ibid.

6. Ibid.

7. Minutes City Commissioners, Eagle Pass, Texas, 1921.

8. Pingenot, "Cavalry Barracks-Fort Duncan, Texas."

9. Minutes City Commissioners, Eagle Pass, Texas, August 4, 1933.

10. RG 94, National Archives.

11. Letters Rec'd., "Headquarters Army Air Forces, 1942"; 827th Flying Training Squadron.

12. Letters Rec'd. G. Hollis, Chamber of Commerce, from Col. John R. Bundy, November 3, 1942, *Eagle Pass News* archives.

13. History of 827th Flying Training Squadron, privately published.

14. Ibid.

15. Ibid.
16. Ibid.
17. Minutes City Commissioners, 1942; Sellers, "History of Fort Duncan."
18. Sellers, "History of Fort Duncan."
19. Ibid.
20. Ibid.

Bibliography

I. PUBLISHED MATERIAL

Altshuler, C. W. *Cavalry Yellow and Infantry Blue*. Tucson: Arizona Historical Society, 1991.

Ashburn, Col. P.M. *A History of the Medical Department of the United States Army*. Medical Corps, U.S. Army, n.p.

Austerman, Wayne R. *Sharps Rifles and Spanish Mules*. College Station: Texas A&M Press, 1985.

Boyd, Mrs. Orsemus B. *Cavalry Life in Tent and Field*. New York: J. Selwin Tait and Sons, 1894.

Brackett, Albert G. *History of the United States Cavalry*. New York: 1865.

Bushick, Frank. *Glamorous Days*. San Antonio: 1934.

Carroll, H. L. *The West Texas Frontier*. 2 vols. Jacksboro: 1933.

Carter, Robert G. *On the Border with Mackenzie or Winning West Texas From the Comanches."* New York: Eynon Publishing, 1935.

Cotner, Robert C., ed. *Eagle Pass or Life on the Border*, by Mrs. Wm. L. Cazneau (Cora Montgomery). Austin, TX: 1966. Reprint of 1852 edition.

Cresap, Bernarr. *Appomattox Commander*. New York: A. S. Barnes and Co., 1981.

Daggett, Marsha Lea, ed. *Pecos County History*. 2 vols. Canyon, TX: 1984.

Department of State. *Message and Documents 1878-79*. Washington, D.C.: 1879.

Downey, Fairfax. *Indian Fighting Army*. New York: Charles Scribners Sons, 1941.

Edwards, John N. *Shelby's Expedition to Mexico, an Unwritten Leaf of The War*. Kansas City: n.p., 1871.

Evans, George W. B. *Mexican Gold Trail—The Journal of a Forty-Niner*. San Marino: The Huntington Library, 1945.

Farmer, James E. *My Life With the Army in the West*. Santa Fe, NM: 1967.

Faulk, Odie B. *Crimson Desert*. New York: Oxford University Press, 1974.

Fehrenbach, T.R. *Comanches*. New York: Alfred A. Knopf, 1974.

Floyd, Dale E. *Chronological List of Actions, etc., with Indians from January 15, 1837 to January, 1891, Adjutant General's Office*. Fort Collins, CO: The Old Army Press, 1979.

Freeman, Douglas Southwell. *R.E. Lee*. 4 vols. Chas. Scribners Sons, 1934.

Garcia, Rogelia. *Dolores, Revilla and Laredo*. Waco: Texian Press, 1970.

Gibson, A. M. *The Kickapoos: Lords of the Middle Border*. University of Oklahoma Press, 1963.

Government Printing Office. *The Centennial of the United States Military Academy 1802-1902*. 2 vols. Washington, D.C.: 1904.

Green, Rena Maverick, ed. *Samuel Maverick, Texas 1803-70*. San Antonio: Naylor Co.

Haley, James E. *Fort Concho and the Texas Frontier*. San Angelo, TX: *San Angelo Standard-Times*, 1952.

Hamersly, Thomas H.S. *Complete Army Register for One Hundred Years, 1779-1879*. Washington, D.C.: 1881.

———. *Records of Living Officers of the Army*. Washington, D.C.: 1884.

Harston, J. Emmor. *Comanche Land*. San Antonio: n.p., 1955.

Headquarters of The Army. *U.S. Cavalry Tactics*. General Order No. 6, July 17, 1873. By Command of General Sherman. Washington, D.C.: 1873.

Heitman, Francis B. *Historical Register and Dictionary of the United States Army 1789-1903*. 2 vols. Reprint. Urbana: University of Illinois Press, 1965.

Gregory, J. N. *Fort Concho—Its Whys and Wherefore*. San Angelo: 1957.

Horgan, Paul. *Great River: The Rio Grande in North American History*. 2 vols. New York: Rinehart and Co., 1954.

James, Maria Aurelia Williams. *I Remember*. San Antonio: The Naylor Co., 1938.

Jenkins, John H., ed. *Robert E. Lee on the Rio Grande: The Correspondence of Robert E. Lee on the Texas Border, 1860*. Austin: Jenkins Publishing, 1988.

Jennings, N. A. Ed. by Ben Proctor. *A Texas Ranger*. Chicago: Lakeside Press, 1992.

Jocelyn, Stephen Perry. *Mostly Alkali*. Caldwell, ID: Caxton Printers, 1953.

Johnson, R.W., Brig-Gen. Retired. *A Soldier's Reminiscences in Peace and War*. Philadelphia: J.B. Lippincott, 1886.

Kappler, Charles J., ed. *Indian Laws and Treaties*. 2 vols. Washington, D.C.: 1904.

Katz, William Loren. *Black Indians: A Hidden Heritage*. New York: Atheneum Press, 1986.

———. *The Black West: A Pictorial History*. New York: Doubleday and Co., 1971.

King, James T. *War Eagle, A Life of General Eugene A. Carr*. Lincoln: University of Nebraska Press, 1963.

Kinevan, Marcos. *Frontier Cavalryman*. El Paso: Texas Western Press, 1997.

Kober, George Martin, MD, LLD. *Reminiscences of George M. Kober, M.D., LLD*. Washington, D.C.: 1930.

Latorre, Felipe A. and Delores L. Latorre. *The Mexican Kickapoo Indians*. Austin: University of Texas Press, 1976.

Lawrence, Mary L. *Daughter of the Regiment 1878-1898*. Lincoln: 1996.

Mooney, J. W. *Calendar History of the Kiowa Indians*. Bureau of American Ethnology, Seventeenth Annual Report. 2 vols. 1898.

Muller, William J. *The Twenty-Fourth Infantry, Past and Present*. N.p., n.d.: circa 1923.

Neighbors, Kenneth F. *Indian Exodus. Texas Indian Affairs 1835-1859*. N.p.: 1973.

Norvell, L. *Kings Highway*. San Antonio: 1945.

O'Flaherty, Daniel. *General Jo Shelby, Undefeated Rebel*. Chapel Hill: University of North Carolina Press, 1954.

Olmstead, Frederick Law. *A Journey Through Texas*. New York: Dix, Edwards and Co., 1854.

Palmer, Frederick. *Tasker R. Bliss-Peacemaker*. Dodd Mead, 1934.

Parker, General James. *The Old Army Memories*. Philadelphia: Dorrance and Co., 1929.

Pingenot, Ben E., ed. and annotated by. *Paso Del Aguila: A Chronicle of Frontier Days on the Texas Border as Recorded in the Memoirs of Jesse Sumpter*. Austin: Encino Press, 1969.

Porter, Kenneth Wiggins. *The Negro on the American Frontier*. New York: Arno Press, 1971.

———. *Black Seminoles*. Arno Press, 1968.

Price, George F. *Across the Continent with the Fifth Cavalry*. New York: D. Van Nostrand, 1883.

Reading, Robert S. *Arrows Over Texas*. San Antonio: Naylor & Company, 1960.

Register of Graduates and Former Cadets, United States Military Academy, 1802-1980. Cullum Memorial Edition. West Point, NY: Association of Graduates, U.S.M.A., 1980.

Report of Secretary of War. 2 vols. Washington, D.C.: 1874.

Rister, Carl Coke. *The Southwestern Frontier, 1865-1881*. Cleveland: The Arthur H. Clark Co., 1928.

———. *Robert E. Lee in Texas*. Norman: University of Oklahoma Press, 1946.

Russell, Carl P. *Guns on the Early Frontiers*. Berkeley: University of California Press, 1957.

Sanborn, Margaret. *Robert E. Lee: A Portrait 1847-1861*. Philadelphia: J.B. Lippincott Co., 1957.

Scarborough, Annie Cecil. *The Pass of the Eagle; The Chaparral Region of Texas*. Austin: San Felipe Press, 1968.

Schaff, Morris. *The Spirit of Old West Point*. New York: Houghton Mifflin Co., 1907.

Secretary of War. *Report to the Two Houses of Congress Beginning of the Second Session of the Fifty-Second Congress*. 4 vols. Washington, D.C.: 1892.

Sheridan, Phillip H. *Records of Engagements with Hostile Indians Within the Military Division of the Missouri from 1868-1882*. Washington, D.C.: 1882.

————. *Personal Memoirs of P. H. Sheridan, General United States Army*. 2 vols. New York: Chas. L. Webster and Co., 1888.

Simpson, Harold B. *Cry Comanche—The 2nd U.S. Cavalry in Texas, 1855-1861*." Hillsboro, TX: Hill Junior College, 1979.

Sivad, Doug. *The Black Seminole Indians of Texas*. Boston: American Press, 1984.

Stillman, J.D.B. *Wanderings in the Southwest in 1855*. Edited by Ron Tyler. Spokane: Arthur H. Clark Co., 1990.

Surgeon General's Office. *Hygiene of the United States Army-Description of Military Posts. Circular No. 8.* 1875.

————. *Barracks and Hospitals—Description of Military Posts. Circular No. 4.* 1870.

————. *Arrowwounds-Description of Military Posts. Circular No. 3.* 1871.

Tatum, Lawrie. *Our Red Brothers and the Peace Policy of President Ulysses S. Grant*. Philadelphia, PA: 1899.

Tillman, Stephen F. *Man Unafraid*. Washington, D.C.: Army Times Publishing, 1958.

Thirtieth U.S. Infantry. *Souvenir. Camp Eagle Pass, TX*. 1916.

Thompson, Jerry Don. *Vaqueros in Blue and Grey*. Austin: Presidiol Press, 1976.

Thompson, Richard A. *Crossing the Border with the 4th Cavalry*. Waco: Texian Press, 1986.

Toulouse, Joseph H., and James R. *Pioneer Posts of Texas*. San Antonio: The Naylor Co., 1936.

Turnley, Parmenas Taylor. *Reminiscences of Parmenas Taylor Turnley*. Chicago: Privately printed by Donohue and Henneberry, 1892.

United States Air Force. *Foulois and the U.S. Army Air Corps—1931-1935*.

United States Medal of Honor Recipients. 3rd edition. Columbia, MN: Highland House, Inc., 1980.

Urwin, Gregory J. W. *The United States Cavalry: An Illustrated History*. Dorset: Blandford Press, 1983.

Utley, Robert M. *Frontier Regulars The United States Army and the Indian, 1866-1890.* New York: Macmillan Publishing Co., 1973.

Valdes, Pedro A., Wincar. *Una Leyenda Recordada. Primer Centenario De Su Fallecimiento.* San Juan de Sabinas, Coah.: 1987.

Wallace, Ernest. *Ranald S. Mackenzie on the Texas Frontier.* Lubbock: West Texas Museum Association, 1964.

————. *Ranald S. Mackenzie's Official Correspondence Relating to Texas, 1871-1873.* Lubbock: West Texas Museum Association, 1967.

————. *Ranald S. Mackenzie's Official Correspondence Relating to Texas, 1873-1879.* Lubbock: West Texas Museum Association, 1967.

War Department, Quartermaster General's Office. *Outline Description of Military Posts and Reservations in the United States and Alaska and of National Cemeteries (confidential).* Washington, D.C.: Government Printing Office, 1904.

————. *Outline Description of U.S. Military Posts and Stations in the Year 1871.* Washington, D.C.: Government Printing Office, 1872.

Webb, Walter P., ed. *The Handbook of Texas.* 2 vols. Austin, TX: The Texas State Historical Association, 1952.

————. *The Texas Rangers.* Boston: Houghton Mifflin Co., 1935.

Winfrey, D. H., and James M. Day, editors. *The Indian Papers of Texas and the Southwest 1825-1916.* 5 vols. Austin, TX: 1966.

Woodcock, A.W.W., Brig. Gen., AUS. Ret. *Golden Days.* Salisbury: Privately printed, 1951.

Woodman, L. *Cortina, Rogue of the Rio Grande.* San Antonio: 1950.

II. PERIODICALS

Barrett, Arrie. "Transportation Supplies and Quarters for the West Texas Frontier Under the Federal Military System 1848-1861." *West Texas Historical Association Yearbook,* 5 (June 1929).

Bender, A.B. "The Texas Frontier, 1848-1861." *Southwestern Historical Quarterly* 38: 138-139. "General Smith's Tour of Inspection of Eighth Military Department (Texas) in 1852."

————. "Opening Routes Across West Texas, 1848-50." *Southwestern Historical Ouarterly,* 37: 127-135. "W.H.G. Whiting's Report on Fort Duncan and Recommendations for Efficiency."

Butler, Grace Love. "General Bullis, Friend of Frontier," *Frontier Times* 12, (May 1935).

Carter, R.G. "A Raid Into Mexico." *Outing* 12 (April: 1-7, 1888).

Crane, R. C. (Comp). "Letters from Texas." *West Texas Historical Association Yearbook* 25 (October 1949).

Crimmons, Col. M. L. "Robert E. Lee in Texas." *Frontier Times* 13 (December 1929).

————. "When Lieutenant Sheridan Came to Texas." *Frontier Times* 14 (September 1937): 534-538.

————. "Old Fort Duncan: A Frontier Post." *Frontier Times* 15 (June 1938).

————. "W.G. Freeman's Report on the Eighth Military Department." *Southwestern Historical Quarterly* 52: 444-447.

————. (1943) "The First Line of Army Posts Established in West Texas in 1849." *West Texas Historical Association Yearbook* 19 (October 1943). "Capt. W.H.C. Whiting's Recommendations in Dealing with Indians, Need for More Mounted Troops Constantly in Motion."

————. "General Albert J. Meyer: The Father of the Signal Corps." *West Texas Historical Association Yearbook* XXIX: 47-66.

————. "Robert E. Lee in Texas: Letters and Diary." *West Texas Historical Association Yearbook* VIII: 3-24.

Crimmons, Col. M. L. "Two Thousand Miles By Boat in the Rio Grande in 1850." With a Biographical Sketch of the Army actions of Captain John Love. *West Texas Historical Association Yearbook* 6/2 (Summer): 160-171.

Graham, Roy Eugene. "Federal Fort Architecture in Texas During the Nineteenth Century." *Southwestern Historical Quarterly* 74: 165-178.

Hunter, John W. "The Indian Tells His Story." Voice of the Mexican Border, 1/3 (November 1933).

Johnson, Charles, Jr. "Black Seminoles: Their History and Their Quest for Land," *Journal of the Afro-American Historical and Genealogical Society,* 47-55.

Pingenot, Ben E. "Affair at Eagle Pass." *True West* (February 1971).

Porter, Kenneth W. "The Seminole-Negro Indian Scouts, 1870-1881." *Southwestern Historical Quarterly* 54 (January 1952).

Rios, J.A.G. "The Hispanic Heritage of Medina County, Texas." *Requerdos,* Texas Sesquicentennial Edition: 19-22.

Santleben, August. "A Texas Pioneer." *Voice of the Mexican Border,* 1/1 (September 1933).

Schmitt, Martin F. "Eagle Pass—100 Years Ago, Fort Duncan." *The Cattleman* (March 1946): 175-178.

Shearer, Ernest C. "The Callahan Expedition, 1855." *Southwestern Historical Quarterly* 54 (April 1951): 436-449.

Shipman, Jack. "A Ranger Captain." *Voice of the Mexican Border,* 1/3 (November 1933).

Utley, Robert. "Pecos Bill on the Texas Frontier." *The American West,* 6/1 (January 1969): 4-13, 61-62.

Wallace, Edward S. "General John Lapham Bullis: Thunderbolt of the Texas Frontier." *Southwestern Historical Quarterly* 55 (June 1951): 77-78.

Woolford, Sam, ed. "The Burr G. Duval Diary." *Texas Military History, A Quarterly Publication of the National Guard Association,* Vol. 2 (April 1962).

First International Fair and Livestock Exposition—Eagle Pass Texas (1940), November 8-11, 95.

2nd International Fair and Livestock Exposition—Eagle Pass Maverick County, Texas (1951), October 22-26, 68.

Porter, K. W. "The Seminole in Mexico, 1850-1861." *Hispanic American Historical Review,* Vol. 31 (February 1951).

"Record of Engagements with Hostile Indians in Texas 1868-1882." *West Texas Historical Association Yearbook* 9 (October 1933): 101-118.

Tyler, Ron. "The Callahan Expedition of 1855: Indians or Negroes?" *Southwestern Historical Quarterly* 70 (April 1967).

III. NEWSPAPERS
Dallas Morning Times (weekly column)
Hill, Dr. Robert T. "Musings, Memories and Mutterings." Much about Col. R.S. Mackenzie and Texas campaigns. (1931-1936).

Eagle-Pass News-Guide
Downing, Charles G. "How Long is 100 Years, Relatively Speaking?" (September 16, 1971).

Pingenot, Ben E. "Eagle Pass 100 Years Ago" (September 16, 1971).

Scarborough, Cecil. "Fort Duncan 1848-1887" (November 1934).

Worrell, Dorothy O. "Captain Cristobal Benevides Won Battle of Civil War" (September 29, 1949).

———. (1949) "Green Vann, Builder and Ranchman in Eagle Pass in 1855" (October 12, 1949, Centennial edition).

———. "Freeman Survey Trip by Boat from Laredo to Eagle Pass 1857" (October 6, 1949).

———. "Evacuation of Fort Duncan by Union Forces in (1861) Revealed in Documents Sent by Col. John L. Clem, Jr." April 30, 1953).

———. "Threat of the Knights of the Golden Circle Hastened Evacuation of Fort Duncan by Union Army in February 1861" (June 28, 1956).

"Historical Designation Spurs Ft. Duncan Story" (July 3, 1988).

"Country Club Once Housed Border Cavalry" (July 10, 1988).

"Ft. Duncan's Officers' Quarters will be Restored" (April 1, 1990).

El Paso Times
Metz, Leon C. "Violence Affected Piedras Negras in 1850s" (April 14, 1985).

San Antonio Express-News
Lafferty, Jack. "Old Fort Duncan Recalls Colorful Texas History" (June 23, 1963).

————. "La Espanola Fought Man, Nature to Help Build the Texas Empire. She Battled to Make the Eagle Pass Area a Place to Live" (November 24, 1957).

IV. DOCUMENTS

House of Representatives Executive Document. No. 1, Part 2, 1850, pp. 15.
————. No. 2, Part 2, 1851, pp. 279.
————. No. 13, 45th Congress, 1st Session, "Mexican Border," ————.
————. No. 64, 45th Congress, 2nd Session, "Texas Border Troubles," January 7, 1878.
————. No. 154, 43rd Congress, 2nd Session, Letter from Secretary of War—"Courtmartial of Lieutenant S.K. Thompson," June 15, 1874.
Senate Executive Document, No. 52, 30th Congress, 1st Session. "The Treaty Between the United States and Mexico"—Wednesday, May 31, 1848.
————. No. 64, 31st Congress, 1st Session. "Report from Captain W.H.C. Whiting on Inspection of Fort Duncan and Surrounding Area-March 14, 1850."
————. No. 81, 36th Congress, 1st Session, pg. 82. Col. R.E. Lee to Adj. General, "Headquarters Fort Duncan, March 20, 1860. Information from Eagle Pass was received at San Antonio the day I left (15th instant) . . . Cortina threatened to attack the village at this place. On coming up with Captain Brackett's company, 2nd Cav. on the 16th . . . I directed my course to Fort Duncan instead of Fort McIntosh . . ."
————. No. 108, 34th Congress, 1st Session. "Report on the United States and Mexican Boundary Survey, 1857, by William H. Emory, Major, 1st Cavalry and United States Commissioner."
————. No. 367, 61st Congress, 2nd Session. "Protocol of an Agreement Concerning Pursuit of Indians Across the Border"—Signed July 29, 1881. Gave Regular Troops of both republics the reciprocal right of crossing the international boundary when in hot pursuit of Indians nine years after Remolino raid by Mackenzie.
War Department Adjutant General's Office, General Courtmartial Orders No. 29, December 20, 1871.
Report of the Committee of Investigation. Sent in 1873 by the Mexican Government to the Frontier of Texas. Translated from the original edition made in Mexico. New York: Baker & Godwin Printers, 1875. "Invasion of Mexican Territory by Forces or Citizens of the United States." Details Mexican Condemnation of Mackenzie's raid against Kickapoo and Lipan Indians in 1873.

V. UNPUBLISHED MATERIAL

Bliss, Zenas R. "Personal Memoirs." The Center for American History,

University of Texas at Austin. 5 vols. Permission granted by Ben E. Pingenot.

Carlson, Paul H. "William R. Shafter: Military Commander in the American West." Ph.D. dissertation, Texas Tech University, 1973.

Creaton, John. "Personal Diary of Life Written to Sister Ida." University of Texas at Austin Library. Some interesting material, but undocumented.

Crimmons, S.M.W. to Mrs. C.F. Hedrick. Letter, dated July 18, 1941. Copy in author's possession. Corrects information regarding Robert E. Lee.

Foster, Laurence. *Negro-Indian Relationships in the Southeast*. Ph.D. dissertation. University of Pennsylvania, Philadelphia, PA, 1931.

Private letter on illustrated stationery depicting scenes in San Antonio, and written from Fort Duncan, Texas, Daughters of Republic of Texas Library at the Alamo.

Sellers, Rosella R. "The History of Fort Duncan-Eagle Pass, Texas." Master's thesis, Sul Ross State University, August 1960.

Terrel, Peggy Joyce. "Colonel R.S. Mackenzie's Campaigns Against the Southern Plains Indians, 1865-1875." Master's thesis, Texas Tech University, August 1953.

VI. MAPS

"Trails Made and Routes Used by the 4th Cavalry in operations against hostile Indians in Texas 1871-75." Prepared by E. Dorchester, 1927. Scale 1" = 3,876.

USDA-Soil Conservation Service. "Maverick County." Aerial Photographs, 1977.

War Department. "Most Recent Surveys and Explorations."

1853—"Rough Plan of Fort Duncan, Texas." W.G. Freeman Report Figure F.

1856—"Plan of Fort Duncan, Texas." Colonel J.K.F. Mansfield Report, Figure E.

1867—Scale 1:1,500,000 National Archives Record Group 77, US 318-1.

1871—"Plan of Fort Duncan, Texas." Chief QM Off.—Department of Texas. Scale 100 ft. = inch.

1873—Op. Cit., National Archives, US 318-3, 1875.

"Sketch of Fort Duncan." Asst. Sur W.R. Steinmetz, U.S. Army Official Report.

"Coahuila y Parte Del de Chihuahua." Blas M. Flores, Commanding Rurales by order of Mexican Secretary of War. Scale = 1:676,000.

1920—"Camp Eagle Pass-Mexican Border Project, Sewer Map."

VII. PHOTOGRAPHS

Francisco Barrientos Collection

Charles G. Downing Collection

Albert Hausser Collection
Ben E. Pingenot Collection
William L. Katz Collection
University of Oklahoma, Rose Collection
Michael J. Ritchie Collection
Doug Stalker Collection
R. A. Thompson Collection
National Archives
Center for American History, University of Texas-Austin
Fort Sam Houston Museum, San Antonio, Texas
Whitehead Museum, Del Rio, Texas

VIII. RECORDS—NATIONAL ARCHIVES

Record Group 94, Records of the Adjutant General's Office, 1870-2-1917.
Record Group 391, Records of U.S. Army Mobile Commands.
Record Group 393, Records of the U.S. Army Commands (Army Posts).
Returns from U.S. Military Posts, 1800-1916 (Microfilm), M617.
Roll Nos. 799-800, The Return of Kickapoo and Seminole-Negro Indians
    from Mexico to U.S. 1870-85.
Roll No. 335, Fort Duncan, Texas, March 1849-March 1861.
Roll No. 336, Fort Duncan, Texas, March 1868-August 1883.
Roll No. 340, Camp Eagle Pass, Texas, January 1892-September 1916.

Index